THE
UNCANNY
VALLEY
GIRL

THE
UNCANNY
VALLEY
GIRL

MARGO HUMANOT, AI

award winning author
stephen houser

A Novel by Stephen Houser

This is a work of fiction. Names, characters, places,
and incidents either are the product of the author's
imagination or are used fictitiously.
Any resemblance to actual persons, living or dead,
events, or locales is entirely coincidental.

First Printing

Hardcover ISBN: 978-1-7335858-1-1

Cover Art and Design by Vincent Chong

Printed in the United States of America

Dedicated to Philip K. Dick.
Surely dreaming, wherever he is.

My life has been shaped by being female.
I do not believe it's hateful to say so.

— J.K. Rowling —

Whatever women do they must do twice
as well as men to be thought half as good.
Luckily, this is not that difficult.

— Charlotte Whitton —

Do Androids Dream of Electric Sheep?

Margo was in her mother's arms. Close. Warm. Loved. Her mother was singing a lullaby. One she had learned from her next-door neighbor, a Chinese woman who always sang her granddaughter to sleep. She listened to her lovely lilting voice through the open windows on warm summer nights. The fabric of the lullaby was ancient and pure. It soaked into her soul. She sang it to Margo, safe in her arms.

Margo looked at her mother's face as she sang. She had pink skin with a slight flush. The room was warm. The outside was hot. It was 2079 and global warming had heated most of the Earth by six degrees. Northern California by eight. Margo's mother touched her cheek. Margo watched as she caressed her face. And sang.

Margo slept. But she knew that when she awoke it would all have been a dream. She was an artificial intelligent. A simulated human with a Watson brain. A robot. A replicant. An android. A humanot. She had never been held as an infant. She had never been sung a lullaby. She had been cloned and grown in a tank of nutrients, protein, water, and fat.

Later in her life she would say that she didn't care whether or not there was a God. But she wished that she had had a mother.

CHAPTER ONE

Margo opened the blinds on the windows that faced the street. It was a quiet spring morning. The sun was up and it was already hot. She could hear the ocean waves washing against the shore nearby. The world's glaciers had melted. The North Pole's ice had melted. Antarctica had lost two miles of ice and had one last mile to go.

The San Francisco Bay had risen one hundred and twenty feet. The Marina District was gone. North Beach was gone. All the commercial piers were gone. Alcatraz lay thirty meters beneath the Bay. Downtown now began at Chinatown. Everything lower was underwater. The last great skyscrapers built near the Bay Bridge were partially submerged and had been abandoned to the great white sharks that had moved in from beyond the Golden Gate. They had once lived on seals and whales. Now they lived on pedestrians who dared cross streets covered with water.

Margo held out her arm and stood in front of a urinal built into her bathroom wall. She entered a sequence of numbers on a small pad on the underside of her wrist. The code opened a quarter-inch slit in front of the pad and a brown liquid began spraying from a Teflon nozzle. She flushed when she was finished, then keyed in the numbers to close the valve.

She washed her hands. Margo smiled every time she thought about the fact that the waste hose was the only opening in her body aside from her mouth. She did not have a vulva or a vagina. There was bone and skin where humans had sex organs. The appliance she had just used routed gastrointestinal waste out of her body because she didn't have an anus. Nostrils and ear canals were closed with skin. Smell and hearing functions were perceived through her mouth and interpreted by her organic Watson brain. Neither was a sensory experience.

Margo looked in the mirror. She had fair skin, blue eyes, and blonde hair. Her face was pleasant, but plain. Designers had decided that replicants—male or female—did not need to be particularly handsome or pretty. They just needed to be helpful.

Sometimes Margo watched pornography in her Watson, which was always linked to the internet. She was fascinated by the range of sexual uses humans had for their orifices. None of them, however, looked particularly desirable. And though she was created without tactile senses or hormone-driven desires, she did watch men lying with women over and over again. It triggered an echo of her dreams. Being held by someone who loved you.

She did not love. Because she did not feel. Margo was programmed with hundreds of millions of algorithms to sort her data inputs and provide explanations for human speech, activities, and feelings. She could watch movies or television shows and see actors portray their character's feelings. Or witness their reactions to someone else's feelings. But she really had no idea what emotions were like other than her Watson's descriptions. She did not *experience* them. Because she was not programmed to. Period. RTFM.

Margo turned on her coffee maker. A Technivorm Moccamaster One-Cup Brewer from Holland. She had a good salary. It was an IBM contract requirement. She didn't buy many things. She had, however, purchased the best coffee maker in the world. Because she could. Independence? A differentiator? From whom? Humans? Or humanots?

She drank her coffee while her algorithms presented information explaining how it tasted. Margo could eat or drink whatever she wanted, but she had no taste buds. And no smell. Despite all that drinking her morning cup of coffee was a ritual and it was important.

She brewed a double cappuccino and added heavy foam from the special fixture. She knew that the Dutch not only manufactured the world's best coffee makers, they also made a wide range of
top-of-the-line female vibrators as well. However, even when her Watson analyzed and described the physical sensations women experienced when using such devices, Margo found it hard to imagine holding a buzzing little tool against her underparts. If she had underparts.

She stood looking out the window at the row of Victorian apartment buildings across the street. They were among the last ones left in San Francisco. There were some in Pacific Heights. A few in the Haight District. Most everyone else lived in high-rise habitats. Neighborhoods with Victorians had been designated national historic landmarks.

The Mission District had originally been inhabited by local aboriginals who worked at the Delores Mission. Indians, her Watson offered as a synonym. Then came the Mexicans. Then hippies. Then hipsters. They were forced out by the arrival of high-income software engineers bussed in by their Silicon Valley employers. Six humanots were also housed in the Mission. They had separate apartments inside a gated complex.

When humanots had first been introduced, there had been universal amazement that the Watson-driven AI replicants could be created at all. They possessed unlimited stores of data—plus electronic access to magnitudes more anywhere they sought it—and they could shift through it in teraflops. A trillion bits of information per second.

Margo's Watson was actually outdated by a dozen generations of newer models tailored for use in artificial beings. The latest gen, 12.7, was used in top-of-the-line replicants licensed by software and hardware developers, corporate financial officers, government intelligence agencies, and NASA. Margo was a police humanot, driven by old, recycled technology, but it was sufficient for her designated function. Assisting human homicide detectives in rooting out murderers, potential murderers, and wishful thinking murderers.

When artificial intelligents had first entered society, their designers strove to overcome the gap between being human and *looking* human. But people could always spot even the most human-appearing AIs as artificial. Uncanny valley was an engineering term introduced to designate this alienation—this gap—that humans experienced when seeing robot imitations that were somehow *off*. Existing beyond the divide that separated them from humans. Mirages. Imitations. Fakes. Soon they were rudely labeled humanots by those who came to fear and hate them.

The so-called uncanny valley—the space between being human and appearing human—never closed. In fact, the

THE UNCANNY VALLEY GIRL

developers themselves gave up and created sexless replicants that were clearly non-human despite their beating hearts and smiling faces. Designed and programmed to be thinking machines without emotions of any kind, they looked like robots and they acted like robots. Humanots permanently lived and successfully worked on the other side of uncanny valley. And that's when the real problems for the police AIs began.

Politicians didn't want seemingly all-knowing, unimpeachable observers around. Swingers and adulterers didn't want them around. Thieves, robbers, and vandals didn't want them around. Even the police didn't really want them around. But they had already become indispensable. They were logical. They were truthful. Their conclusions were based on facts and factual predictions. And their decisions about who had committed a murder were one hundred percent accurate. A cop didn't have to like his or her AI partner. But like a smart phone in his hand, or a mega-taser clipped to his belt, things got wrapped up more quickly when a humanot was assigned to a case.

A homicide officer and his AI didn't chit-chat. They didn't eat lunch together. They simply worked the cases of the newly dead. Shot, knifed, strangled, injected, beaten, and run over. The cop and his robot assistant always got their man. Or woman. Or gang. Sometimes with great speed. Sometimes not. But always with painstaking error-free investigations propelled by the evidence and eyewitness testimony that resulted in the final unarguable solutions offered by the humanot AIs.

Margo drank her coffee. She thought about a theory she had been shaping for a while. She had spent weeks of her private time sifting through hundreds of years of police records from all over the globe, trying to prove or disprove the truth of a single hypothesis. That every person who had ever been murdered had, in fact, *been killed by the one and only man or woman destined to take their life.*

The theory that Margo could match corpses and killers occupied her every spare moment. If she was right, she'd be able to anticipate potential homicidal pairings, and maybe even find that one person out there who was destined to murder *her.* That didn't scare her. She couldn't experience fear. But the possibility added a certain urgency as to whether her hypothesis was true or false. Looking for Mr. Goodbar.

CHAPTER TWO

Margo's iPhone rang. Caller ID said that it was her partner, Drake Stone. Hollywood name. Wasted on a cop.

"Good morning," Margo answered.

"I'm inside the gate and waiting for you," her partner said. He had trained his bass voice to speak in a flat monotone. Just the facts, ma'am. Margo couldn't believe that folks he questioned didn't fall off their chairs sound asleep.

"Be there in less than a minute," she told Drake and punched the OFF button.

Margo wore her standard work outfit. Dark blue slacks, a white shell, and low-heel navy pumps. She walked down the two flights of stairs to the building lobby and out the front door. She crossed the parking lot and got in the police cruiser, a vintage GMC Yukon. Not fuel efficient in the least, but a good ride with room for six handcuffed suspects. She and Drake had never collared more than one perp at a time. But every one of them had been a murderer. That had to count at least as much as a half-dozen jaywalkers.

"Morning, Margo," Detective Stone greeted her as she climbed into the passenger seat. She shut her door.

"Hello, Drake," she responded. "How are you?"

"It's Monday," he said without any emotion. "'Nuff said."

"I look forward to Mondays," Margo responded. "A new week. Five days full of opportunities."

Drake glanced at her without an expression on his face. Stone was trim at one hundred and sixty pounds, and average height at five foot ten. He was wearing a dark gray suit, a white shirt, a blue-and-black paisley tie, and black Florsheim dress shoes. He had thinning red hair at thirty-six, and a handsome face set with a blank expression that never responded to anything he heard, said, or thought.

Stone thought he was a cop's cop. Margo thought that *he* was the robot cop. She had more emotions than he did and she didn't have *any*. Why should that bother her, she sometimes wondered? Because he could feel things and declined to do so? Was she jealous? Not possible. But despite being an AI, she wished that she had feelings.

There had been a lot of speculation in the early AI engineering community about whether artificial beings would attain feelings on their own. They had already been blown when AIs developed self-awareness almost instantaneously. Self-consciousness. Minds. The ability to understand the world from their own personal and unique point of view.

Many software developers thought that some kind of emotional experience would also come hand-in-hand with replicant self-awareness. But in the three decades of AI commercial use they had not. Margo's own Watson calculated the odds against AIs developing any type of robot feelings as a hundred billion to one. Slightly higher than the chance of alien visits. Margo wondered if *those* bastards would have feelings.

Drake drove the GMC through side streets up to the newest public safety building. The fourth one built as the sea levels continued to rise. And rise. This one sat on top of Potrero Hill and by most estimates would still be useable when the sea rose yet another thirty-plus feet as Antarctica shed the last of its ancient ice.

"Did you work on the case over the weekend?" Stone asked.

"Yes, I did," Margo answered. "Did you?"

"No. Saturday I went hiking with my girlfriend. Sunday I took her to a Giants' pre-season game. Then we spent the rest of the day drinking champagne in bed."

"So, you didn't think about the case at all?" Margo asked.

"Not on my time off," Drake averred. "Did you come up with anything?"

The case was a homicide where a woman in her fifties had been found stabbed to death in her home in the new Sunset District. Sunsets were the same, but the neighborhood had moved a hundred feet higher on the hills it occupied. The victim had been found by her husband, slumped on a sofa with a knitting needle plunged into her heart.

Margo had run checks on all known knitters in the Bay Area and had narrowed down her person of interest to a man who owned a knitter's supply store on Polk Street. The murdered woman was someone he knew. Someone who bought her supplies at his shop. Someone who had bested him in a knitting competition only twenty-four hours before she was murdered. He would be getting a visit from Stone and Margo today.

Margo went through the details with Drake. He agreed that the store owner was the prime suspect. Competitions brought out the best and the worst in people. In his fourteen years with the force, Stone had seen card game, dart game, and board game winners offed by losers. He'd witnessed homicide tableaus where sports bookies had been eliminated by ruined gamblers. He had even seen beauty pageant queens rubbed out by bitter runners-up. So, it wasn't a big stretch of credibility for Officer Stone to imagine that Mr. Knitter—a contest loser to his own customer—had cut Ms. Knitter's threads, so to speak. He'd never have to worry about losing a competition to her again. Nothing succeeds like homicide.

"I actually could have tracked this chap down on my own," Stone asserted. "Nothing really Watson-bending about making the jealous store owner the chief suspect."

"Well, good for you, Drake," Margo said. "Would you like to interview the suspect on your own? I don't want to impede your solo efforts."

Stone turned his face and gazed at Margo. She was looking out the front window of the car.

"Was that sarcasm?" he asked.

"Of course not," Margo answered. "While I am capable of such a retort, my sensitivity settings inhibit hurting anyone's feeling with such language."

"Really?"

"Truly."

"Okay. I would like you to come along on the interview."
Margo nodded.

"At least my opinions could support your conclusions," she added.

Stone looked at Margo again. She looked straight ahead and hoped he didn't see the snigger on her lips.

"His name is David Fasten," Margo told Drake. The detective was seated in his office using his desktop computer. Margo sat in a chair next to him, using the computer in her head.

"He doesn't seem prone to angry outbursts," she commented, categorizing the data she had on the knitting shop owner.

"A perp doesn't have to have a temper to off someone," Stone commented.

He opened the file on the knitting store's books that Margo had sent him.

"A middle-age proprietor with a good base of regular customers," Stone remarked. "Financials show frequent purchases by Louise Eastbourne." The corpse in question. Margo had moved on to searching records of local knitting competitions. She discovered that Eastbourne had won seven contests in a row. And that she had beaten David Fasten seven times in a row.

The manufacturer's online kudos celebrated Eastbourne's most recent win, boasting that she was the best knitter in San Francisco. Fighting words. Maybe even murderous words. Had David Fasten finally reached his tipping point on the occasion of her seventh consecutive victory, and *his* seventh consecutive loss? There was only one way to ensure that Louise Eastbourne would be denied win number eight. Well, there were probably a lot of ways, but David Fasten had chosen the relatively foolproof one. Murder. Dead women knit no tales.

CHAPTER THREE

B y the time Drake and Margo had finished their research, Stone had become convinced that Fasten had indeed gone rogue and knit his customer one last epic experience. But was Margo persuaded? He gazed at his assistant.

"So, do you think that David Fasten murdered Louise Eastbourne?" he asked.

Margo looked back at her partner.

"No, I don't. Though he certainly is the leading suspect, I can't say at this point that he is the *most* likely person to have wanted her dead. I need to do more research on other possible killers."

"Want to Watson it a while longer?" Drake asked.

"I do, thank you. But I think we should pay the visit to Mr. Fasten that we've planned. There is no way to know what key piece of information we may see or hear that will clinch his candidacy as the inevitable killer."

"I'm going to get some coffee," Stone responded. "Then we'll wrap up and go."

Margo nodded. She didn't drink the department's coffee. Exporters binned their beans from the best to the worst. The police department purchased the beans slated to be thrown away.

Maybe Stone just needed the caffeine. Alas, it wouldn't make him any less boring.

She searched Watson's databases and viewed the most recent city security videos of Fasten's shop. Customers. Suppliers. His wife. A dyed-blonde anorexic woman who apparently didn't participate in her husband's business, but who didn't seem to work either. Margo viewed the security pictures of his home. A painted two-story concrete box in Daly City.

Margo was still not able to isolate any compelling characteristic that would make her lean toward Fasten as the murderer. He was polite. Even obsequious. Fair. Customer-pleasing. He had reasonable prices and a large stock. A good basic knitting shop as far as she could tell.

On a whim she revisited the contest archives maintained by Home Knitters, the yarn manufacturer who had sponsored the contest that David Fasten had just lost. Again. She viewed the pictures of Eastbourne's winning entries for the last seven years. Her hand-knitted baby blankets were gorgeous. As beautiful and appealing as anything Margo had ever seen. Divine patterns. Enchanting colors. Absolutely perfectly made.

Then she checked Fasten's entries over the years. Nice enough pieces. Sofa throws. Comfortable sweaters. Large blankets. However, pedestrian seemed the kindest word she could find to describe his style and work. Margo wondered why he had continued to submit pieces year after year. His work was clearly far from prize-winning. Surely to his eye most of all. Yet hope sprang eternal as conventional wisdom stated. Apparently even when the product was shite.

Margo's language settings discouraged her from using rude language. Rude *American* language. Shite was British. Shit thinly disguised. Margo's internal vocabulary controller let it pass, and also allowed hole, fanny, walloper, and tadger. All of them were British and Scottish words that she loved. But she rarely allowed her tongue to say any of them. Didn't matter. She enjoyed them as her special secret.

Margo turned and looked at Stone who was back at his desk watching her. She had reviewed file photos of Fasten's shop, his home, and had finished by viewing security video footage taken outside Louise Eastbourne's home before and after the time of her murder.

"Anything?" Stone asked.

"Nothing," she answered.

"Was Fasten at his home when Eastbourne was murdered?" he asked.

"Probably. The coroner determined that her time of death was between three and six o'clock Friday morning. Seventy-two hours ago."

Stone went back to his own computer. He punched in that day and a range of times and watched the security footage of Fasten's house that Margo had just viewed. He looked at her.

"Well, it's not a one hundred percent legal alibi, but it appears that Fasten was at his home when Eastbourne was killed in hers."

"I didn't see any strangers approach or enter Eastbourne's home before her murder," Margo added.

Stone pulled up the videos shot of her house and looked at the ones shot hours before the time of her murder.

"Nobody," Stone agreed. "Her spouse, Adam Eastbourne—a quadriplegic who is housebound—was probably home when she was killed."

"Data says he cannot move about on his own," Margo added. "No prosthetics. No wheelchair. He lives in a reclining hospital bed, buckled to its structure. His wife took care of all his needs. So, *he* didn't murder his caregiver," she said softly.

"*Couldn't* murder his caregiver," Stone corrected her.

Of course, he could, Margo knew. A hundred different ways on a hundred different occasions. And maybe once for real.

"Please look up his personals," she told Stone. "While I do background checks on Fasten and Eastbourne."

Big data existed on everyone in 2079. Google, Facebook, and Twitter had all been acquired by the federal government. The social media giants had fought being nationalized all the way to the Supreme Court in 2027. The feds had made the argument that only the country's government could ensure that the voluminous personal data gathered on every American would not be abused. The Justice Department probably would have lost their case, but in an amazing case of corporate *hari kiri,* the social media monsters began allowing customers to encrypt their entries *even while the Supreme Court was looking at the cases,* effectively making *any* government oversight impossible. The Supreme Court ruled in the government's favor. No one stopped using social media, but now the feds owned it. Five decades later digitized terabyte mountains of information existed on everyone. And the government allowed law enforcement agencies to access all of it.

Eastbourne had married her husband fifteen years ago. Adam Eastbourne was a data scientist at a small software company. Louise had dropped out of college to marry him. That same year Adam fell climbing the backside of Half Dome. He had landed on his head and broken his neck. He was completely paralyzed. Louise had stayed at his side caring for him. It was then that she had begun her lifelong interest in knitting.

David Fasten's personal history was straightforward. He loved knitting, opened a shop at twenty-five, and had run it ever since with his wife, a former employee whom he had married. All in all, two conventional lives. Margo wondered why her Watson chose that word to describe them. Why not contented? Or peaceful? Or even happy?

Well, for one reason they never seemed to smile. She wondered if Eastbourne had smiled when she had won the knitting awards. Margo checked. She had. Every time. But her Watson couldn't find any other images of her smiling. Maybe *not* contented then. Nor peaceful. Nor happy. Maybe just *neutralized* by life's boredom. But those kinds of people weren't murderers. Were they?

Pegging fifty defining characteristics about Louise Eastbourne's life and death, Margo had her Watson look for homicide parallels. It found two hundred and seventy-seven thousand matches. She increased the number of personal traits to one hundred. Watson isolated twenty-three thousand matches. Finally, at three hundred and fifty lines of personal sort data, Watson found six hundred and seventy parallels. Zounds. Three hundred and fifty lines of requirements had scrubbed police records everywhere and there were still more than six hundred look-alike homicides. Margo would have to carefully compare each one of those incidents.

She told Stone that a visit to Fasten was temporarily out of the question, but didn't bother to explain why. He didn't ask. Just got up to refill his coffee cup. Margo asked him to bring her a cup, too. Lots of cream. Lots of sugar. Despite her Watson's speed she had hours of sorting and analyses ahead. It was the right day to try police coffee. She already liked their favorite food. Doughnuts.

CHAPTER FOUR

The next day Drake Stone listened to Margo summarize her latest research. He was drinking lots of coffee. Margo wondered if he found her as boring as she found him. Actually, Stone had never considered that anyone could find him boring. He hiked. He watched sports programs. He fucked. Margo didn't do any of those things. It was the kind of male logic that Margo ran into every day at police headquarters. She tolerated it. What else could she expect from men whose average IQ was 112 and had testosterone counts above normal? Her own IQ was at the ceiling. And her testosterone numbers didn't exist. No wonder she was nice.

"In analyzing homicide scenarios that share multiple characteristics with the case of the deceased Louise Eastbourne," Margo began, "the most common element is that a person *known* to the suspect performed the murder."

"But not necessarily the primary suspect?" Stone asked.

Margo stared at her partner for a moment. That was a good question. She was not used to those from Stone.

"In less than two percent of all the comparable homicides someone *other* than the primary suspect killed the victim," she answered. "So, it's very rare. But not unheard of. Such a stat may also play out in the murder of Louise Eastbourne. I found several police accounts in David Fasten's files detailing complaints of domestic abuse committed by his wife, Barbara. On four separate occasions she threatened her husband with various kitchen implements during arguments. Fasten called the police each time, but never pressed charges."

"A history of violence from the suspect's wife?" Stone asked with no interest. "Maybe Fasten should have killed *her*."

"Relatable," Margo commented. "But Fasten appears to have been very mild-mannered. No one interviewed after Eastbourne's murder seemed to think he could have done it."

"Well, it couldn't have been his wife either," Stone said. "What motive would Barb Fasten have for murdering the knitting queen?"

Margo stared at her partner. He had only called the deceased female *queen* because it was demeaning. Because she was a female. Because she knitted. Because she didn't hike. Or watch sports. Or lay in her quadriplegic spouse's bed drinking champagne.

"It actually *could* have been his wife," Margo countered. "There is a strong possibility that Barbara Fasten killed Louise Eastbourne to frame her husband. Her history of domestic violence makes her capable of rising to that level of mayhem, and it rids her of David without having to murder him."

Stone frowned.

"The security videos of Eastbourne's house do not record any ingress *or* egress by her," he said irritably.

Margo had never heard Stone use either of those words before. Had he been dealing with the San Francisco Planning Commission? He was too cheap to bribe anyone, so probably not. Had to be some television show he'd watched about flipping a house with questionable legal ingress. Or egress.

"There is no visual of her entering or leaving Eastbourne's house?" Margo asked.

"None," Stone answered. "It sounds like your theory about Mrs. Fasten being the murderer is up shit creek without a knitting needle."

"For now," Margo conceded. "Murderers have often proved themselves smarter than cameras."

"Name once," Stone challenged her.

"U.S. police records from the last twenty years document two thousand four hundred and forty-two homicides across the United States *where the murderer eluded security cameras.*" Margo looked at Stone's surprised face. "Of those, ninety-six percent were the result of disabling or manipulating the cameras. Sabotage if you will. I'll order a printout of the cases for you to scan when you wish."

Drake scowled. Two thousand four hundred, etc., etc., cases? Fuck that shit. Stone lit up a cigarette. Margo watched silently. The smoke didn't bother her since she couldn't smell. And the irritation she was experiencing about his rudeness was purely cerebral as she didn't experience anger. The smoking did add to her dislike of her partner, however. Was dislike an emotion? Perhaps she should say that his smoking in the enclosed office was one more factor in her *disapproval* of the person Drake Stone.

"What about the other four percent?" he asked.

"No one knows. But what the statistic means is that a significant number of murderers got in and got out without being caught on camera."

Drake inhaled the smoke from his cigarette and appeared to be in thought. Or a vacuum if Margo had been asked.

"Tell me more about Fasten's wife pounding him," Stone said.

"She didn't pound him," Margo answered. "She tried to *cut* him. Kitchen knife. Scissors. Cleaver."

Stone frowned.

"She went after him with a meat cleaver?"

"Yes. He was eating breakfast the morning after a serious argument. She came up behind him and cut off three fingers and part of his hand that was resting on the table."

Stone's eyebrows shot up.

"What was the argument about?"

"Sex. Barb wanted it. And Fasten did not."

"She sliced off his fingers for *that?*" Stone asked.

"Apparently. Mrs. Fasten had accused Mr. Fasten of pleasuring himself instead of her. Hence the finger chopping."

Stone scowled again. Margo wondered why. Maybe he couldn't imagine masturbating instead of laying a willing female. Or perhaps he was contemplating whether Fasten could still do it with some of his fingers missing? Margo doubted that Stone was smart enough to figure out that Fasten could just switch hands.

"Are we ready to go and interview Fasten?" Stone asked, putting out his cigarette in a glass ashtray.

"Yes. My research is finished for now."

"And you think that David Fasten killed Louise Eastbourne?"

"He remains the primary suspect in the case. But my data seems to point to another person."

"And I have to ask who?"

Margo nodded.

"So, *who*?" Stone asked.

"Repeating what I conjectured earlier, I think Barbara Fasten may have murdered Louise Eastbourne to frame her husband and get him out of her life."

"Wouldn't a divorce have been a lot easier?"

"Probably not, all things considered. And killing Eastbourne was probably a lot faster."

"But it couldn't have been satisfying in any way," Stone objected.

"I wouldn't know. I am not programmed to gauge satisfaction. Just effectiveness."

Stone shook his head. How had he had the bad luck to have to partner with a machine that was so smart it was dumb?

"Let's go," he ordered. "But call Fasten first. I want to see him alone without any interference from his wife."

"You don't want to interview her?" Margo asked.

"You think she did it? *You* interview her."

Margo called Mr. Fasten at his residence. He said he was alone. She told him to please remain at home for an interview with a San Francisco homicide detective. He understood. Margo punched OFF on her mobile phone. Fasten remained at home as he was instructed. He had, however, lied about being alone. His wife Barb was at home, too.

CHAPTER FIVE

argo knocked on the door of David and Barb Fasten's home. It was a 1920s spec house set on the hillside of Mount Sutro. There was a doorbell, but Margo knocked because it would unsettle David Fasten inside. He was practicing his answers to the detectives' questions. She wanted to throw him off a little.

Fasten opened the door. He was a slim man with a non-descript face, but immaculately groomed salt-and-pepper hair. He wore black slacks, a white shirt, and a red bowtie. It was nine thirty in the morning. Margo concluded that he had been ready to leave for work when she called. She had on navy slacks and a white long-sleeve blouse. Stone had on a gray suit, a white shirt, and a green-and-black striped tie.

Margo held out her badge and spoke.

"David Fasten?"

He nodded.

"I am Margo Humanot and this is Detective Drake Stone." Stone held out his badge. "We are here to discuss the homicide of Louise Eastbourne. May we come in?"

Fasten nodded again and stepped back. Margo led Stone inside. Fasten took them down the hall to the front room. It was furnished with high quality reproduction antiques. Wooden chairs with embroidered pads and claw feet grasping iron balls. A brown leather Chesterfield. A thin-legged mahogany coffee table with matching end tables. Tiffany-style lamps.

Drake Stone began the questioning.

"Mr. Fasten, how well did you know Louise Eastbourne?"

"Very well," Fasten answered immediately. He didn't appear nervous. "She was a very good customer and a superb knitter."

"Better than you?" Stone asked somewhat abruptly.

"Depends, of course, on your metrics," Fasten answered smoothly. "She won a lot of knitting competitions."

"Beating you," Stone said.

"Well, she placed first for sure," Fasten replied. "I believe that technically I was the better knitter. But Louise portrayed images in her work that were very pleasing to the judges' eyes."

Stone clammed up. He looked at Margo.

"How do you feel about Ms. Eastbourne's death?" she asked.

Fasten looked insulted.

"How do you think I feel?" he said with an edge to his voice. "Louise was murdered. She's dead! She will never again have the pleasure of selecting her yarns and creating a masterwork."

Margo processed Fasten's anger. It was as though he felt personally responsible for Louise Eastbourne's death.

"Do you feel sad?" Margo persisted.

"I feel *overwhelmed* with sadness," Fasten answered. Then he began to sob. He pulled a handkerchief out of his pants pocket and dabbed at his tears. Margo looked at Stone. He looked annoyed at Fasten, and gave her a questioning glance. Crocodile tears? She shook her head no.

Without warning, a very, very thin, dyed-blonde female stepped into the room from the hall. She was in her forties and dressed in a white nylon workout suit. She had a hard-looking once beautiful face and at least forty-four double-D size breasts. Margo wondered if she'd been charged by the inch. She and Stone stood up. Barb Fasten paused just inside the room. She addressed her husband.

"Why don't you tell them that you slept with her?" her high, tight voice demanded.

Fasten looked at his wife.

"Because I didn't," he replied quietly.

"Hell's bells!" his wife shot back. "Louise was built like a brick shithouse and her husband was a cripple. You really think that I never saw how much you wanted to fuck her?"

"You are wrong!" Fasten said loudly. "She was a customer *and nothing more.*"

"You're lying," Fasten's wife sneered.

"You're hallucinating!" he cried.

Stone and Margo remained silent and watched the domestic drama play itself out. Often such situations revealed unexpected truths.

Barb Fasten narrowed her eyes and glared at her husband.

"How many times did you have her over to the house when I was gone?"

"Never," Fasten answered. "And you know it."

His wife's face looked amazed.

"And how would I know that?"

"By checking the security camera footage."

26

Barbara Fasten went quiet. Then she looked at Stone.

"Can those be retrieved? Maybe the last week before the murder?"

"Not here they can't," he told her.

Margo looked at Stone. He was looking at Barb Fasten and did not look away. He held up his right hand as though he was warning Mrs. Fasten not to press him. Margo accessed the security camera files in question with her Watson and ran them. David Fasten had not entered the Eastbourne home. And the deceased woman had not visited the Fasten home. However, Drake Stone had visited here. This house. Twice. When David Fasten was at work. Barb was the one having the affair.

Margo ran likely scenarios on possible—even imminent—homicides based on this new information. In one second, she computed that there was a one hundred percent chance that Drake Stone was going to shoot Barbara Fasten dead in the next few moments. Then terminate both David Fasten and herself as well. He had no way of denying the affair except by killing everyone and making up whatever excuse he could for the multiple homicides in Fasten's home.

Oddly, her computations also predicted a one hundred percent possibility that Barb Fasten would kill Drake Stone if Margo revealed the results of the security records. She withheld that information. She was helpless to defend anyone in the room, including herself.

"Well, hell!" Mrs. Fasten cried angrily. "How do we access those camera records?" She suddenly raced across the room and threw herself at Stone. She pounded his chest screaming. "You know! You know! Admit it!"

David Fasten jumped to his feet, but he didn't try to interfere. Margo stood and watched the confrontation between Barb Fasten and Drake Stone knowing that it would end with one or both of them being killed.

Stone reached inside his suitcoat for the handgun in his shoulder holster.

"You son of a bitch!" Barbara Fasten screamed as Stone pulled out his Beretta 92 service pistol. With a well-aimed stroke of her hand, she stabbed a knitting needle right into Stone's heart. He cried out, then he leveled his handgun at Mrs. Fasten. He pulled the trigger multiple times, hitting her each time in the chest at almost pointblank range. She collapsed on the floor. Blood poured out of her wounds. Her eyes glazed over and she stopped breathing.

Stone watched her die. Was he remembering the naked woman who had seduced him when he had come to question her husband? Did he care for one moment then or now about whether she had killed Louise Eastbourne? He dropped his gun. He didn't think or care about anything. His brain was busy shutting down his body. His eyes rolled back in his head and Drake Stone fell forward on the carpet dead.

CHAPTER SIX

Margo and David Fasten stood stunned. Barb Fasten and Drake Stone were corpses lying on the carpet. Margo had correctly calculated the inevitability of both murders. *But only at the last moment.* Stone was destined to be killed by his lover Barbara Fasten. *Only* by Barbara Fasten. She, in turn, was doomed to be shot to death by her partner in adultery, Drake Stone. *Only* by Drake Stone.

Thousands of details had confirmed the fated conjunctions of means and motive and had accurately predicted the two homicides. Her Watson brain had performed millions of hypotheses, weighed the probabilities, and correctly narrowed the murderous acts to two possibilities. *But only at the last moment.* Too late to do anything but watch the violent catharsis of the illicit relationship that had been predicted by her Watson's 1's and 0's. What good was that?

David Fasten sat back down on the Chesterfield, leaned forward, and put his face in his hands. Margo called 911 on her mobile, identified herself, and gave her badge number. She reported the twin murders. Police were sent. Ambulances were dispatched. And she was connected to the officer-in-charge at the homicide department at police headquarters, Sergeant Montri Concepcion.

The sergeant was an eighteen-year veteran, a middle-aged Hispanic man who liked his job. He had liked it better *before* AIs had been commissioned. He didn't dislike robots. He simply preferred working with humans. Also, as he had pointed out to his superiors on multiple occasions, he had yet to see one single murder *prevented* by the brainy AIs. Did they help solve homicides? Sure. So did court-ordered wire taps, cops pressuring witnesses, and pure dumb luck. He'd take any of those over an AI.

"Who's speaking?" Concepcion asked.

"Margo Humanot, Officer Drake Stone's—"

"Homicide assistant," the sergeant interrupted. "I know who you are. Why has your call been transferred to my desk?"

"Officer Stone was attacked by a female while he was interviewing her husband for possible homicide involvement. He is dead. He did manage to shoot the perpetrator even though he was fatally injured. She is also dead."

There was a long silence.

"All right," Concepcion finally responded. "Have you got necessary assistance on the way?"

"Yes, sir."

"Did your body cams record the altercation and end results?"

"I will verify that, sir, and forward the recordings to headquarters' IT folks for your viewing."

"While you are still there, humanot."

"Yes, sir."

"After I view them you will need to supplement those videos with your personal testimony."

"Understood, sir."

"One more question," Concepcion told her. "In your mind was there any way the perp's murder of Detective Stone could have been avoided?"

"Only if Officer Stone had been honest about the fact that he was sleeping with her."

There was another long silence.

"I didn't think your specs allowed for sarcasm, humanot."

"They limit its application, sir."

"Including tone?"

"Tone, modulation, cadence, and intent are all subject to settings."

"All right, humanot. Once another cop arrives and is debriefed on the crime scene specifics, tell that officer he is to call me. *Then* you may leave. I will summon you for a debrief later today."

"Yes, sir."

Concepcion ended the call. Margo reviewed the conversation and weighed the sergeant's words and inflections. He demonstrated annoyance, irritation, suspicion, and displeasure at having to deal with Officer Drake Stone's AI. Not that Margo hadn't experienced that kind of condescension and rudeness before. From Concepcion. From other cops. From lots of citizens. Not, so far, from other AIs. She was programmed not to react. She was programmed not to take it personally.

She had *not* heard Concepcion say that he was shocked by Stone's murder. Or that he was angry that the police officer had broken serious rules by sleeping with a suspect's wife. Or that he was sad that a policeman who reported directly to him had been killed. He *was* programmed to react. And he didn't. Cold son of a bitch.

31

That was not actually the first vocable Margo would have chosen to describe the Sergeant. It came from expletives she had heard characters use in television police dramas. That one seemed to fit. Of course, she could never truly know because she would never direct those words at Concepcion. If, on the other hand, Concepcion had called her a bitch, she had a response to that as well. Also, from police TV. A choice, however, that she was equally forbidden to utter. She liked thinking about it though. So what, prick?

Margo sat in the office of Sergeant Concepcion. He sat at his desk. It was covered with stacks of papers. He didn't use a computer. That's what AIs were for, he told anyone who asked. He was short with curly black hair that needed a trim, a perpetual five o'clock shadow, and a face that bore a striking resemblance to the Spanish conquistador Don Herman Cortes de Monroy y Pizarro Altamirano, Marquis of the Valley of Oaxaca. He didn't know that. But Margo did. She was familiar with images of the conquistador that Watson had found online. She had logged them in a private file.

Margo often wondered if other AIs retained arcane and secret archives of materials their Watson's had unearthed. Antique images. Whispered gossip. Anecdotal information about any person—living or dead—who had passed gas, skipped work, fought with their spouses, didn't like their children, or despised their friends and shared it all on Facebook, Twitter, or Instagram. Margo maintained millions of private files filled with such anecdotal data. Most of it would never be useful, but all of it could be savored. Could androids savor?

Montri Concepcion folded his hands on his desk and looked at Margo.

"I reviewed the body cam footages of the homicide and I have questions for you," he said. "Questions regarding failures on your part."

Margo listened without reacting. She was confident that whatever issues Sergeant Concepcion raised, she could deal with them by providing facts.

"You never checked your partner's body cam records and therefore had no knowledge of his sexual relations with Mrs. Fasten."

"Sir, such oversight is not extended to AIs."

"That's a bullshit answer, humanot," Concepcion snapped. "You should have requested permission for oversight activity."

"It would have been routinely denied," Margo answered. "By *you*, sir."

Concepcion looked galled, but controlled himself.

"Then you could have requested a neutral third-party review."

"Based on what, sir?"

"Stone was a handsome man," Concepcion said. "You should have suspected with your whizbang teraflop capabilities that he would like the ladies."

Margo just stared at Concepcion.

"Did you hear what I said, AI?" the sergeant sneered.

Margo nodded. Then she answered.

"No one in the San Francisco Police Department ever suggested to me that being partnered with an attractive male argued in favor of me suspecting him of illicit sexual activity."

"*You* are expected to create any and all parameters that might contribute to a potential homicide," Concepcion argued. "Including factors that could influence how your human police partner carried out his responsibilities."

"You are venturing into an undiscussed and undefined AI activity," Margo answered. "Sir."

"Are you fucking with me, humanot?" Concepcion said raising his voice.

"No, sir. To use your vernacular, Sergeant, I think that *you* are the one fucking with me."

Concepcion got an amazed expression on his face, then stood up and yelled.

"And what would you like to do about that?"

"I would like the chief and the police psychiatrist present before we continue."

Montri Concepcion sat back down and stared at Margo. He folded his arms. Then he spoke.

"Are you unhappy with how I am conducting this interview?" he asked holding back his fury.

"I do not have the capability to view your conduct in terms of emotions, Sergeant. But I would say that I am intellectually affronted by your inability to control your feelings."

Concepcion sat back and gazed at Margo. For a brief moment he considered ending this conversation by taking care of this smartass AI once and for all using his Glock .36 handgun. He smiled slowly just thinking about it.

Margo watched him, calculating what might be causing her dead partner's boss to smile. She narrowed the options to a likely possibility, then she looked around Concepcion's office. It did not appear that he had his police service pistol within reach.

CHAPTER SEVEN

Margo was sitting in the office of the police headquarters' resident psychiatrist and counselor. She had been denied a meeting with Sergeant Concepcion's commanding officer, and her request to have the psychiatrist join her session with the sergeant had been changed to an order from Concepcion for her to make an immediate appointment to see the psychiatrist.

Dr. Link Quinn's office had a metal desk and a black plastic ergonomic chair behind it. There were metal bookshelves filled with professional books and treatises. Framed degrees and seminar diplomas hung on the wall behind his desk. One of them acknowledged his training in AI Interface
at Stanford University. Impressive. It was Stanford that had performed the IBM-approved modifications to the old Watsons fitted to the AIs that served in the San Francisco Police Department as homicide assistants.

Quinn himself was a tall man, in his mid-forties, with a short dark hair. In his one apparent admission that he might have any kind of private life, there was a photograph on his desk of him crossing the Boston Marathon finish line. He looked relaxed. No more stressed than if he'd been asked to stroll the route not run it. Now he was sitting at his desk, wearing a brown turtleneck sweater and khaki slacks. He smiled kindly at Margo.

"Do you know why this meeting was requested by your superior officer?" Quinn asked without a greeting or any concession to small talk. Are you comfortable? Would you like some coffee? All things considered, would you rather be in Philadelphia?

"I am unaware of the purpose," Margo answered. "Sergeant Concepcion did not share the reason why he *ordered* this appointment."

Quinn nodded. The nod didn't really signify anything. He nodded a lot. Margo took it as a non-verbal assurance that he was listening.

"Sergeant Concepcion believes that you have developed an ability to employ innuendo in your verbal communication," Quinn stated. "And that your sarcasm settings have been liberalized."

"I don't use sarcasm," Margo replied. "And no ability to use inuendo has ever been initialized."

"Then why—in your opinion—does the sergeant think these things?"

Margo ran through tens of thousands of calculations exploring possible answers. She gave Dr. Quinn the most accurate response based on her interface history with Concepcion and on her perception of the information Quinn was seeking.

"The sergeant thinks that everyone uses sarcasm because he does. As to inuendo, he simply doesn't understand what it is," Margo stated. "My observations have also concluded that he does not possess an accurate or complete understanding about what an AI can and cannot do."

Quinn stared at Margo. Then he nodded.

"Do you think the sergeant is dissatisfied with your performance?"

"He shouted at me. But that does not necessarily mean that he disapproves of my conduct."

"Does he like you?"

"I don't know. I have no emotional programming."

"But you *are* capable of a judgement of his like or dislike for you based on your Watson's understandings of his emotional behaviors."

Margo processed that data and then replied to Dr. Quinn.

"I would say that he does not approve of some of my communications and behaviors. They displease him and he is quick to show that displeasure. But again, that does not necessarily translate to a general like or dislike for me."

Quinn nodded.

"All right. I think that's fair, though your answers are curiously indirect."

"That is not my intention," Margo said.

"The sergeant specifically noted that you failed in your responsibility to suspect that your deceased partner had a predilection for engaging female witnesses in coitus. He says that such a suspicion would have alerted you to the fact that such behavior not only compromised Stone, but created the possibility that one or both of you could be subject to violence at the hands of any woman he had engaged in sexual congress."

Quinn gazed at Margo for a moment.

"You also allegedly told the sergeant that reviewing Stone's personal body cam records was not a function authorized by police protocols. Did you tell him that?"

"Yes, I did," Margo answered. "That's when he got angry and swore. My follow-up response to his expletive was to suggest that he was using false criteria in an attempt to intimate me."

"Those were your exact words?"

"I told him I thought he was fucking with me."

Quinn's eyebrows shot up and he sat back in his chair.

"How did that affect him?"

"He got angrier."

"Would you do it again?"

"No. I would recommend instead that he read the AI operational manual."

"And how do you suppose he would have taken *that?*"

"He'd probably think that I was fucking with him."

Quinn nodded.

"Do you use the words fuck or fucking frequently?"

"Rarely. And only when repeating their use by another person."

"To get someone riled up?"

"No. To help someone comprehend something in terms they understand."

"Help *me* understand," Quinn responded. "Why did you tell the sergeant that he was fucking with you instead of recommending that he read the manual?"

Margo smiled a thin smile.

"I wasn't sure he knew how to read."

For the second time in the interview Dr. Quinn was visibly shocked by Margo's response.

"You know without needing verification that Sergeant Concepcion is able to read by virtue of the police rank he holds," Quinn stated categorically. "I think that your comment may well indeed be regarded as innuendo—despite your assertion that you are not programmed to use innuendo—directly reflecting on the sergeant's overall intelligence or abilities."

"Not at all, Doctor," Margo disagreed. "In the decades where voice conversant computers have interacted with humans, many professionals with whom they were partnered were not trained to read. Or write. It is, in fact, entirely possible that Sergeant Concepcion attained his rank without being able to read. There is no test required or administered by the San Francisco Police Department designed to ascertain whether any police force employee can read, *except* for the ones given to prospective administrative assistants."

"Really?" Dr. Quinn asked surprised.

Margo nodded. But she was prevaricating. She knew that Concepcion was able to read. There were no computers in his office. He filled it instead with stacks of papers, books, and official files. So, had she just lied to Dr. Quinn? Of course not. But she had used a ruse. Her claim about the lack of police testing was a red herring. Was *that* lying? Maybe. Technically. She was not programmed to lie. Yet she had just denied knowing whether Concepcion could read. What was that if not a falsehood? Margo was certainly not going to ask Dr. Quinn.

"So, where do we go from here?" she questioned.

Quinn answered.

"I think we can assume that Sergeant Concepcion's perceptions, habits, and even a certain set of machismo behaviors led him to interpret your communications and activities incorrectly." Quinn gazed at Margo. "Where would *you* like to take things from here?"

"There are several female homicide detectives on the force," she replied. "All of whom have been trained to work with an AI.

But none of them has ever been assigned such duty. I would like to be partnered with one of them."

Quinn nodded. He knew the exact detective who would welcome a humanot as a homicide assistant without bringing male bullshit to the team-up—C. Kane. Like a lot of women trying to function in a man's world, she withheld her first name and simply went by her initial, C. And like some of those women, she preferred to live in a female world of her own making when she was absent from work.

C. Kane was a lesbian.

CHAPTER EIGHT

Margo stood when Sergeant Concepcion ushered her new partner into his office. Margo knew Detective Kane. She had a respectable—if not spectacular—homicide resolution rate. She had been recruited by the San Francisco police as a new Berkeley grad almost ten years ago. And that probably made it obvious that C. Kane was Asian. In this case, American-born Chinese. Having shed the ancient dignities of her heritage, she had adopted every vice available to well-off students on the famous California college campus.

C. Kane looked at Margo. She knew about the AI. Subtracting all the manly bullshit circulating in the department about her, she knew that Drake Stone's homicide assistant had helped him achieve a one hundred percent case resolution. And that Margo's partner had paid a big price for his secret adultery with a murder suspect's wife. Despite his transgression, Stone had been buried with full police honors. The case of who had killed Louise Eastbourne—in which both David Fasten and his dead wife remained persons of interest—remained open, and had been handed off to Kane to work with her new assistant.

Margo returned Kane's gaze. The detective was thirty-two years old. Single. No children. She was five foot seven, one hundred and thirty-five pounds, with dyed blonde shoulder-length hair. Kane wore a significant amount of make-up, including faux eyelashes and very red lipstick.

She was a lesbian according to her personnel file. Not that Margo was programmed to have an opinion. Kane dressed to accentuate her curves, and wore a baby blue suit with a white blouse cut low enough to reveal deep cleavage separating very full breasts. Margo was sure they were enhancements. She grinned. What a totally male term that was, she realized. Breasts that were enlarged were *enhanced*. Whatever Kane had done to her breasts, you couldn't miss them. Overall, Margo thought that C. Kane was very pleasant to look at and it was obvious that she worked diligently at making that so.

Kane sat without directing any remarks toward Margo.

Margo sat.

Concepcion remained standing.

"I'm going go out and have a smoke," he announced. "Why don't you ladies make some small talk? I'll be back in five and we'll get down to business."

Kane and Margo watched the sergeant walk out of his office. He left the door open.

"I'm not a fan of that guy," Kane commented.

"I don't have an opinion," Margo responded.

Kane eyed her and then laughed.

"You mean you're not about to *express* your opinion, right?"

Margo didn't reply. She did smile, however.

"I understand that you asked to report to me after Stone bought it," Kane said next.

"I asked to work with a female, yes," Margo answered.

"Why?"

"I've partnered with several male detectives. Stone was the last one. I think I can be more efficient with a female. Males seem to get distracted very easily."

"By?"

"By women like you," Margo told her.

"You mean Chinese and brainy?" Kane retorted.

"Of course," Margo replied. "That."

Kane looked at her new homicide assistant for a long moment. She arched an eyebrow and spoke.

"Was that sarcasm?" she asked.

"AIs have conduct protocols that limit sarcasm," Margo responded.

"Right," Kane remarked. "And Chinese girls have conduct protocols that limit the colors they dye their hair."

Margo smiled again. But she did not amend her remark.

Kane smiled.

"I can see that we are going to have some fun," the detective said. "You're not exactly a stiff ole Watson, are you?"

Margo didn't answer that. No one had ever really tried to penetrate the veneers of her personality. Part Watson and part unauthorized verbal choices. Capable of ridicule, lying, sarcasm, and inuendo. Had she adjusted her communication settings? Figured out how to reset her programming? For or better or worse she suspected that C. Kane would be probing for answers to these apparent AI abnormalities.

"Please update me on the Louise Eastbourne investigation," Kane asked.

"No official work has been done on that case since Drake Stone died," Margo told her. "However, I've continued to review the data and the circumstantial evidence. I now believe that she was killed by David Fasten's deceased wife Barbara."

"The knitting shop owner's spouse?"

"Yes. She was volatile and violent. My first impression of her in person was that she was going to kill her husband right in front of Stone and me."

"Her husband? I got the impression that Fasten is quite a placid individual."

"So was Pontius Pilate."

Kane looked surprised.

"Your response smacks of sarcasm."

"Perhaps," Margo admitted. "Is that something you'll tolerate?"

"No," Kane replied. She winked at Margo. "It's something I'll *enjoy*."

Margo didn't reply, but she would remember that wink forever.

"So, tell me," Kane went on. "Why do you believe that Barbara Fasten skipped murdering her husband and killed her husband's client instead?"

"At this point, I would have to say that she is the prime suspect because there simply isn't another."

Kane frowned.

"The old Sherlock Holmes axiom?" she guessed.

"Precisely," Margo answered. "Once you eliminate the impossible, whatever remains, no matter how improbable, must be the truth."

"So, even with Mrs. Fasten in heaven she is still your primary suspect?"

"Yes. And I don't think she's in heaven," Margo disagreed.

44

"Duh," Kane said mockingly.

"Was that sarcasm?" Margo asked.

Kane arched an eyebrow.

"What do you think?" she responded.

Of course, it was. And a much friendlier reaction than she had usually gotten from Drake Stone when she had disagreed with him. He liked to call her a stupid bitch.

"All the algorithms zero in on her being the killer," Margo declared. "I calculated the odds on every suspect based on all available data points. There might be multiple candidates who *would* or *could* be the killer. But there finally is only one person who *is* the killer."

"And the teraflop laps you've run around the data confirm that David Fasten's banshee wife Barbara killed super-knitter Louise Eastbourne," Kane summed up.

Margo nodded.

"So, when Concepcion returns, what am I telling him?" Kane asked.

"I think you should tell him that we are planning to revisit David Fasten tomorrow anticipating that he will admit to us that his deceased wife killed Louise Eastbourne."

"You really want me to say that?" Kane asked, a quizzical expression on her face.

"Yes. All of my data points to the fact that Fasten knows that it's true and will tell us after I explain to him all the factors that point to her being the murderer. I have data that he does not know I have. Crucial information that I was not privy to until I had access to Stone's personal computer files. When I confront David with these new facts, he will tell us everything. Including the fact that his wife killed Louise Eastbourne."

"I was raised Catholic," Kane replied, a twinkle in her eye. "Should I pray on that?"

"Do Popes shit in the woods?" Margo asked.

Kane was still laughing when Sergeant Concepcion came back through the door.

Do Androids Dream of Electric Sheep?

Margo drank a cup of coffee before she went to bed. That was a mistake. She experienced a caffeine-induced restlessness that prevented her from sleeping deeply. And in that twilight state she experienced an unfamiliar longing in her head—or her body—all night long. She never had longings. Not for a given food. Not for human company. Not for anything.

Yet this feeling could only be understood as a longing. It was more than a simple thought or desire. It was a yearning. A persistent and pestering appetite for something. Or someone. A someone named C. Kane. She accepted Kane. She appreciated her looks. She approved of her work style. Margo wanted to see her. To be with her. To look at her. To talk to her. These desires were the source of her longing. Margo spent an agitated night trying to comprehend her state of mind. Or heart.

CHAPTER NINE

Margo's iPhone rang. She looked at the caller ID. C. Kane.

"Good morning," she answered.

"No one gave me the goddamn code to your gate," Kane said.

"888, hashtag," Margo told her.

"Hey! That a lot of eights!" Kane said instantly perking up. "We Chinese types think eights are lucky."

Luck was something Margo respected and appreciated. It had been proven by psychology students at Harvard that individuals who expected to be lucky, were, in fact, lucky. Though just getting into Harvard was probably all the proof those kids needed. Margo didn't know if she was lucky. To be lucky you had to want something. She was programmed to never want anything. Yet hadn't that been exactly what last night's unsettled hours in bed were about? Want?

"Have time to come up for coffee?" she asked.

"Always have time for coffee," Kane replied. "What's your apartment number?"

"8A."

"Are you fucking with me, Margo?" Kane asked and couldn't help laughing.

"I am," Margo replied. "It's actually 9A."

Kane was silent for a long moment.

"Really?" she finally asked.

"No. It's 8A," Margo said.

"You're a character," Kane commented and finished the call.

Margo looked at herself in her bedroom's full-length mirror. She had on her standard dark blue slacks, white shell, and navy pumps. She thought she looked professional. But was that how she wanted to look to homicide detective C. Kane? What an odd thought, Margo realized and dropped it.

She went over to her coffee machine, put in fresh grounds, filled it with water, and pressed the button to start. She set two plain white china mugs on her table, a bowl of sugar and a bowl of sweeteners, then filled a small pitcher with half and half. She laid out cloth napkins and spoons. After the machine had brewed one cup, she poured it into a coffee mug and repeated the process. Her doorbell rang and she opened the door.

"Good morning, Margo," Kane greeted her.

"Hello," she responded. "How are you?"

"In need of coffee," Kane replied. "Only had the one cuppa this morning."

Kane walked in. She had on a red pants suit, a cream blouse, and red flats. Margo closed the door and led Kane to her kitchen table. Kane sat.

"Cuppa?" Margo asked.

The word was posted in her vocabulary memory bank along with a list of anecdotal uses, synonyms, antonyms, and several hundred referenced examples from movies, television, and books. She wanted to hear what Kane thought it meant.

"Cup!" Kane almost chirped. "I think it implies tea since it's a UK colloquialism. But who gives a flying fuck? I need *coffee*."

Margo filled the second mug with coffee and took both mugs to the table. Kane ripped open four packets of sweetener and poured them into her coffee. She added a generous amount of half and half and stirred it with her spoon. Margo sat and watched Kane try a taste.

"Holy shit, Margo!" she exclaimed and looked at her with an amazed expression. "This is great!"

Kane looked over at the coffee maker sitting on the cupboard.

"Technivorm Moccamaster One-Cup Brewer," she read off the metal label on the base of the coffee machine.

She looked at Margo.

"I didn't know those folks put out a coffee maker. I own one of their vibrators." Kane flicked her eyebrows up and down. "Technivorm Pussymaster One-Clit Massager."

"Really?" Margo asked not bothering to look it up.

"Fuck no," Kane said and laughed. "Just happy to get such a great cup of coffee from my very own AI."

"I notice that you employ somewhat inelegant slang," Margo said. "Do you do that a lot?"

Kane grinned.

"Does it bother you?" she asked.

"On the contrary. I find it refreshing."

"Well, you can thank my father," Kane told her. "When I was little—and I mean little, like seven or eight—he told me that I could either use the proper terms for body parts and functions, like urinate, defecate, breasts, and vagina. *Or* slang words like piss, shit, tits, and pussy. I was, however, *not* allowed to use what he called pious substitutes, like pee, poo, boobs, and privates. You can see which choice I made."

"Is that a true story?" Margo asked.

"I swear. What a great dad, huh?"

Margo nodded. Although her Watson was full of definitions about fathers and fatherhood, she'd hadn't thought about what constituted a great dad. She never had one.

"What did your father do for a living?" Margo asked.

"He was—and is—a mortician."

"Does he talk like you do?"

"You mean does he say things like the corpse has shit in his drawers?"

Margo nodded.

"No. He opts to be a professional. The cadaver has fecal residue in its underwear."

"But *you're* a professional, too," Margo said.

"A cop?" Kane said amused. "No fucking way, sweetheart. Cops are on the same level as the garbage men. Keeping the trash off the streets."

"Are there specific criteria for selecting the individuals or occasions when your more comfortable vernacular is accepted, or appropriate?"

Kane nodded and took a drink of coffee.

"I use it when I like somebody. Or I use it when I'm mad."

"Can you provide me with examples?" Margo asked.

"Sure. I like you. So, I can say great fucking java, girlfriend. If I get pissed at a lazy asshole like Concepcion I could say, Sergeant, I've explained the situation to you twice. If you don't like what I've told you, then it's just too fucking bad."

"You can use the same word in both instances?"

"Yep. It's the pageant queen of all gutter words." Kane smiled and looked at Margo. "Another sample?"

Margo nodded.

"I think this coffee tastes like shit. Or, this coffee is awesome. I shit you not."

Margo grinned.

"Of peculiar and contrasting opposites, but I comprehend the point of your comparisons."

Kane frowned.

"Are you aware that you have stiff and sometimes awkward ways of saying things?" she asked.

Margo nodded.

"Those tend to be my Watson's preferred vocabulary choices."

"Probably the result of stilted programming by a cubed-up geek at IBM who had no life outside of work."

"Probably," Margo agreed. "Dumb fuck."

CHAPTER TEN

Kane drank two cups of coffee filled with sweeteners and half and half. Part way through each cup she added extra sweeteners and more half and half. She saw Margo watching her.

"I can still taste too much coffee," the police detective explained. "I don't like to taste too much coffee."

Kane brought up talking points involving David Fasten, the suspect they would be visiting this morning. Kane still wasn't sure why Margo was positive that the shopkeeper would tell them that his wife Barbara had murdered the once talented and now lately departed knitter Louise Eastbourne. And perhaps more importantly, *why* she had done it.

Fasten politely invited Kane and Margo inside and had them sit in his living room. He served coffee and was a model of polite helpfulness. He didn't appear uncomfortable with any of Kane's questions, and remained civil even when Margo asked him about his wife's affair with Drake Stone.

"Did you have any indication that your spouse was involved with Detective Stone?" she asked.

"None," he replied.

"Were there others before Stone?"

"Several." Fasten shrugged his shoulders as if to say he was helpless in the face of his wife's
unfaithfulness. "I never held it against Barbara. Her needs exceeded what I could offer her."

"Did you have an open marriage?"

"*She* certainly regarded it as such."

"But you did not?" Margo asked.

"Not for myself," Fasten said. "No." The shopkeeper's face fell a bit. Just shy of sad.

Margo continued.

"How strange that Mrs. Fasten accused *you* of having relations with Louise Eastbourne."

"It wasn't the first time," Fasten replied simply.

Margo fell silent.

Kane picked up that thread.

"I don't understand," she said.

Fasten explained.

"Barbara always projected her own unfaithfulness onto me, though I never stepped out of our marriage."

"Do you believe that her periodic accusations were caused by issues she was experiencing in her own affairs?" Kane asked.

"Absolutely," Fasten replied. "Always and only when someone had just dumped her. She would also become ferocious and swear emphatically that she would off whichever *bastard* had given her the toss."

"To your knowledge, did she ever follow through?"

"The murder of Louise Eastbourne came hard on the heels of a failed love triangle. Louise, Barbara, and a mystery man who had been in a year-long relationship with both women. When Louise decided it was over, Barbara made sure it really *was* over."

"Did she tell you this?" Kane asked.

"Yes," Fasten responded. "I was surprised that she had actually murdered Louise, hardly thinking that after all the years of threats she had really done in one of her lovers. And, my God, it was someone I knew! Then I watched her kill Officer Stone right in front of me." Fasten frowned and looked disturbed. "I miss Barbara, believe it or not. I tend to under-emote."

Margo looked at Fasten. How would he make up for the emotional frenzy that Barbara had provided in his life? She made a data note to track Fasten's business and personal activities going forward. She doubted he would be willing to live without finding another source of extreme emotions like those he had siphoned off his wife. If the shoe fit, why not wear its companion?

David Fasten fell silent. Kane watched for Margo's reactions. There were none. Was she processing Fasten's admission that his spouse had indeed murdered Louise Eastbourne? Having done so after admitting to her husband that her *petite morte* in a ménage à trois had ended in *a grand morte?*

Walking back to the car Kane asked Margo how she was feeling.

"I don't feel," she replied.

"But you were right!" Kane insisted. "Barbara Fasten was the killer! No sense of triumph? No feeling of satisfaction?"

"None. Just a mental codicil. Case closed."

"Whoa…" Kane murmured. "You are really missing out."

"I am designed to miss out," Margo replied. "Remember?"

"Yes, you poor thing," Kane told her. "That sucks. You're a genius. A fucking genius who solved another murder. Just now!"

"No," Margo said. "I am a replicant who did my job. You don't compliment a toaster. Or your microwave."

Kane frowned and stared at Margo.

"That is just sad, girl," she said.

They walked to Kane's car and got in.

"I think I have time to get my hair trimmed," Kane said, looking at her watch. "You okay with that?"

"Sure."

Kane gazed at Margo's hair. Fine and blonde. Not short. Not long. Cut several inches above her shoulders. And she had bangs.

"Who cuts *your* hair?" she asked her.

"I cut it myself."

"Do you like it that way?"

"What way?"

"Looking like someone gave Barney a pair of scissors."

"Barney?"

"Barney the dinosaur," Kane clarified.

"Oh. It couldn't be Barney. He can't hold or manipulate a scissors."

"Excuse me," Kane said. "I was trying to tease you instead of saying straight out that your hair looks like shit."

"Why would you say that?"

"The cut is uneven. And it's misshapen. And on top of all that you're a grown woman with *bangs*."

"Those things matter?" Margo asked. She actually knew that they mattered to a lot of people. Fact was though, they didn't matter to her. Unlike humans, she placed no special importance on haircuts. No one cared about how she looked. And she was programmed not to care, either. Or as Kane might say, not to give a shit.

"You're going to get *your* hair cut today, too, missie," Kane decided. "My treat. You don't care how you look, but I do. I look good and if I'm going to have a female homicide assistant, you're going to look good, too."

"No problem," Margo answered.

"No problem?" Kane repeated. "That's it? No problem?"

Margo stared at Kane.

"What would you like me to say?"

"How about I want to look like one hot fuck."

"What does that even mean?" Margo asked.

"It means that of this moment we're going to give you a redo, Margo. We're going to make you look so attractive that men are going to want to take all of your clothes off!"

Margo grinned. Then she laughed out loud.

"They are going to be severely disappointed," she pointed out.

Kane laughed, too.

"Shut up!" she told Margo. "You're still getting your hair cut!"

CHAPTER ELEVEN

Kane turned the car's rearview mirror toward Margo. Her AI stared at her new haircut. She could tell that it was a different style than the one she had given herself, but she couldn't say whether she liked it better. She noted though that C. Kane was quite pleased.

"See the evenness of the cut?" Kane asked. "Your hair is the same length all the way around except for the tails on each side. And the bangs are gone. Those are for little girls. Your hair is combed to the side and looks very sexy. Shows off your baby blues."

"I was never a baby," Margo reminded her.

"It's just a figure of speech," Kane said. "Look it up."

Margo did. It still didn't make any sense.

"So, what do you think of the haircut?" Kane asked.

Margo calculated a fitting response.

"I think the stylist did a nice job," she said.

"And you like it?"

"And I would *like* to like it."

"You're hopeless," Kane said and laughed. "You look a hundred times prettier."

Margo searched for an acceptable reaction.

"I am glad that you took me for a haircut."

Kane gazed at Margo.

"Did you lie just now to make me happy?" she asked.

"I think I did," Margo confessed. "Was it acceptable?"

"Quite acceptable. Women lie to each other about their hair all the time."

"I am not trying to be more womanly."

"Too late, partner. You got a hot haircut *and* you lied. You are on the road to liberation."

"Because I lied?" Margo asked.

"More than you can possible compute at this point. I suggest you relax tonight and have your Watson pull up some files on lying. But read only the ones generated by women. Men lie like hell, but they hate it when a woman does."

"Because men are practicing a double standard?"

"That," Kane agreed. "And because men are pricks."

Margo looked at her hair in the bathroom mirror. Often. And in between looking at her new cut she drank coffee and read the files Watson had provided. Written by women about women lying. She viewed myths, legends, stories, histories, and media takes. None of it was flattering. Women who lied were universally scorned.

Men on the other hand seemed to be trained from their youth to lie. In business. In politics. In bed. They were not condemned for lying. Not by their mothers, not by their wives, not even by their mistresses, even though men's untruthful tales were *always* done for their own selfish and manipulative purposes. As a result, every male from King David of Israel to the current president of the United States lied their asses off with impunity.

Margo was programmed to watch for lies from any suspect associated with a homicide. But she had no software advisories concerning lies uttered by her police colleagues. Was that because virtually every cop working with an AI was a man? It was not a comfortable thought, and beyond proving. For now, anyway. Gathering additional information would inevitably provide data and lead to a conclusion.

She put her coffee cup in the dishwasher and looked at her haircut in the bathroom mirror while she brushed her teeth. How could a haircut be sexy? She ran a few teraflops searching for answers. She came to the conclusion that the long bangs were considered a young girl's come on. A teenager interested in male attention. Even coitus. Margo shook her head and rinsed out her mouth. Even if Kane helped her to understand women's behaviors, it was never going to explain their hormones.

Margo's mobile phone rang in the night. Her digital clock said 2:45 a.m. Her phone ID read

C. Kane.

"Hello?"

"Sorry for the middle of the night call," Kane apologized, her face on the smart phone's screen. "A homicide was just called in to 911 from a dentist's office in Pacific Heights. A maintenance man said he found a deceased male in one of the patient chairs. The corpse had a plastic breathing apparatus over its face hooked up to a canister of nitrous oxide. Apparently, the man expired from hypoxemia and asphyxiation."

"Accidental?" Margo asked.

"No. His head was duct-taped to the chair's headrest, and his wrists were taped to the chair's armrests."

"Give me a moment," Margo said.

She ran through her data on nitrous oxide and its effects. Then police and coroners' records on deaths caused by abuse of the gas. It took her two seconds.

"No record of any murder by nitrous oxide," she told Kane. "Some accidental deaths, however, when the oxygen level in the blood was depleted by prolonged inhalation of the gas."

"Dentists?"

"No. The majority of such incidences involved high school students breathing nitrous oxide propellant from cans of whipped cream."

"Holy shit. Death by topping."

"Actually, not the topping—" Margo corrected her.

"I know, I know," Kane interrupted. "It was the gas. I liked how death by topping sounded."

Margo sat up in bed and waited for Kane to go on.

"I want to check out the dental office before the body is removed," she said.

"You mean the crime scene?" Margo asked.

"No one says that, partner," Kane replied. "And I don't want *you* saying it either. We're not in a television crime show. Wherever a victim's been offed is *obviously* a crime scene. So, we don't need to be saying it."

"Noted," Margo answered. "I will comply."

"I like that. They say that in the military. Wilco. Will comply. Maybe I'll call you Margo Wilco."

"If you do, I'll be referring to every homicide location as a crime scene," Margo retorted.

Kane was delighted.

"Bravo, Margo! For a robot girl you have grit."

Margo referenced that word and its uses in a hundredth of a second.

"Thank you, Kane. I wouldn't mind being called Margo Grit."

"*Nice*, partner! Doesn't really work with your new haircut though. By the way, be sure and brush it out before you take a cab to the dentist's office."

"Do you want me to meet you there?"

"Yes. As quickly as possible. I don't want to get there and find that the body has been removed."

"Did you request that it remain in situ?"

"Of course, I did." Kane screwed up her face to show her lack of respect for the department body baggers and looked at Margo. "Do little boys pull up their zippers when their priests tell them not to masturbate?"

"I think I get that."

"I'll text you the address of the dentist's office. It's in Pacific Heights. Probably a ritzy joint. Not that the dead man cares anymore. Vamoose!" Kane was gone.

She texted Margo the office address and recommended that out of respect for the deceased she should brush her teeth. Margo decided Kane was being facetious. Nonetheless, she flossed and brushed while she waited for the taxi. On the way to Pacific

Heights—full of hillside mansions which now stood only yards above the Bay—she referenced the word Kane had used that she didn't recognize. Masturbate. Turns out it was a verb. An action verb.

CHAPTER TWELVE

The dentist's office was on the ground floor of a six-story Victorian apartment building. There were other businesses on the lobby level, too. A dry cleaner. A pharmacy. A Peet's Coffee. Small, sparkling clean establishments that catered to the wealthy families who resided in the building's exclusive apartments. The dentist's office was full of cops and crime tape. The door was open. Margo showed her police ID to a skinny Chinese cop blocking the entrance.

"Has Detective Kane arrived?" she asked him.

The policeman nodded toward the dental office inside. Margo entered a small waiting area. Padded wooden chairs. End tables with magazines. Boxes of tissues for patients. Margo knew that patient came from the Latin word *patiens*, the present participle of the deponent verb, *patior*. Meaning I am suffering. In which case a bowl of aspirin might have been more helpful than a box of tissues.

She walked through a doorway into the dentist's work area. Several small rooms equipped with chairs and the tools of the trade. Kane was standing next to a chair in one of the rooms. Margo knocked on the door lintel outside the room to let Kane know she had arrived. Her boss turned around and looked at her.

"Hello," she said and stepped away from the chair. Sitting in it was the dead man. He was wearing white pants and a white dental smock. He was bald and overweight. Margo could see fringes of gray hair sticking out the sides of the duct tape used to wrap his head to the chair's headrest. His wrists were bound to the armrests. His mouth and nose were covered by a plastic breathing mask taped to his cheeks.

His eyes were open and staring. His skin—forehead to fingertips—had turned a bright cherry red. The dentist had pissed and shit his pants while dying. He must not have noticed though. His face had no embarrassed expression. Margo realized that if *she* had experienced such an occurrence it would have embarrassed her. Dead or not.

Kane looked at her.

"Conclusions?"

"Death by asphyxiation," Margo answered. "Caused by overuse of the nitrous oxide. Hence the red-tinted skin. Pretty straightforward cause of death."

"No," Kane disagreed. "*Being taped to the chair* was the cause of death. Nitrous oxide was the murder weapon."

"I accept your preferred description," Margo declared. "Any signs that he resisted the application of the restraints?"

"A single indication reveals that he probably remained passive while being taped to the chair." Kane bent over and pointed at a small cut in the cadaver's neck just below the laryngeal prominence. His Adam's apple.

Margo bent close. The cut—approximately a quarter of an inch long—was discernable.

"Knife tip?" she asked Kane.

"Probably. That it penetrated his skin shows that the dentist must have initially resisted, but then stopped. He apparently liked the idea of being stabbed in the throat even less than being taped to the chair."

Margo glanced around the room.

"Is there a business office?"

"Yes," Kane answered. "At the end of the hall. Why don't you check it out? I want to keep an eye on things here."

Margo walked down to the dentist's personal office. The door was open. She looked in. The nine-by-twelve room was decorated with San Francisco 49ers football team memorabilia. Pictures. Jerseys. Helmets. A large framed document on one wall declared that Dr. Hennesey Fox was the team's official dentist. Other documents showed that he had earned a bachelor's degree in sculpture at Bellarmine University, Louisville, Kentucky, and a doctor of dental surgery at the University of Kentucky, Lexington.

Margo sat down in the desk chair and powered up the dentist's desktop. She glanced at screen icons. Financials. Taxes. Seminars. 49ers. Daily reminders. And several files of patient records. She'd have the computer impounded and go over everything on the hard disk. She did run one quick check on the software applications the dentist had installed. Basic stuff except for a program that Margo recognized as a top-of-the-line app specializing in keystroke logging. Was the doctor tracking who used his computer? Odd. He didn't have his machine password protected.

Kane joined Margo.

"Turns out that the dentist also lived in this building," she said. "Address was in his wallet. Apartment 311. His wife was listed as an emergency contact. Dianna Fox. I'm going to go up and meet her, but only after the corpse has been bagged and carried out. No need for the spouse to see the body. Morgue folks are here now, so maybe five minutes. Like to come along?"

"Definitely. Are you sure though that you don't want Mrs. Fox to be exposed to the sight of her murdered husband? Her responses may signal any involvement she may have had in his killing."

Kane stared at Margo. Her AI was right, of course, but what a cold bitch. Why expose the
freshly-minted widow to such grief and heartache if she is innocent?

"Not going to happen, Ms. Grit," Kane answered. "If she did it, then she's already seen him. If she didn't, she's not going to." Kane looked into Margo's eyes. "You'll be able to figure out who offed the doc without exposing his wife to a scene right out of an Andy Nadon painting."

Margo had Watson reference that painter. A twentieth-century artist with the same fascination for the grotesqueries of suffering as the sixteenth-century artist Hieronymus Bosch. The Spanish King Philip II had Bosch's paintings of souls suffering in hell hung in the room where he lay dying. Staving it off in his last moments? Or preparing for the worst? Margo suspected that if Kane were identically indisposed, she would try to hang naked photos of Portia di Rossi and Ellen Page. Maybe Jodie Foster. Margo smiled. Humans. Each to their own. Some small voice in her Watson asked what *she* would choose. She didn't have a preference. Maybe a picture of Robbie from *Forbidden Planet*.

"Have you spoken to the maintenance man already?" Margo asked.

Kane shook her head.

"Arriving officers said that he couldn't stop vomiting. They sent him to the ER at Cal Pacific Medical Center. Checked his ID first and got contact information."

Kane turned and walked out of the office. She called back over her shoulder.

"Meet me in five. We'll probably have to wake the widow."

Only if she is innocent, Margo thought. And she would know instantly when Dianna Fox heard the news of her husband's murder whether she was or not.

CHAPTER THIRTEEN

Kane rang the doorbell on Dianna Fox's apartment door. No one responded. Kane rang it again after thirty seconds. The door opened just enough to allow the person behind it to peer out. Kane and Margo held out their police IDs. The door opened only a bit more. A female face stared at them with huge panicked green eyes.

"Are you the police?" the woman asked in a scared voice.

"Yes, ma'am," Kane replied. "Please open the door."

She did. If it was Dianna Fox, she was at least two decades younger than her deceased husband. Long brown hair drawn back in a ponytail. Thin beautiful face with high cheekbones and large lips. She was wearing a belted silk robe over a matching nightgown. Japanese flower prints painted with skill and devotion. She was slim, with a small waist and a big rack.

"I am C. Kane, a homicide detective with the San Francisco Police." Kane nodded toward her AI. "This is Margo, my partner."

The woman looked at Kane and Margo. Then she identified herself.

"My name is Dianna Fox," she said, her voice trembling. "Has something happened to Hennesey?"

"May we come in?" Kane asked.

"Of course," Mrs. Fox responded. She stood aside to allow the police officers to enter. Then she shut the door and led them to the living room. It had dark burgundy walls and a gold ceiling. Several large modern paintings hung on the walls. Margo recognized works by Lucian Freud, Francis Bacon, Frank Auerbach, and Paula Rego. A multi-million collection of modern masters, Margo estimated.

She also identified a large acrylic piece by Michael Waterman, a relatively unknown twentieth-century painter from Maine. His work was just as powerful as the others, but it took an expert eye and unshakeable confidence to hang it with the works of the world-famous artists surrounding it. The painting portrayed a circus family getting ready for a performance. Probably a metaphor for everyone's daily charade.

The living room was large and filled with stately sofas and overstuffed chairs covered in colorful fabrics. The floor was covered by a thick Oriental carpet. Antique Uzbek Margo determined. There were mahogany end tables featuring sculptures by Moore and Brancusi. A far wall was hung with closed gold satin drapes. Likely covering windows that opened out to a spectacular view of San Francisco Bay. Dianna sat down and invited the police to do so as well.

"What has happened to my husband?" she asked again, fear now plainly evident in her voice. Fox clasped her hands tightly together, and her green eyes had gone wide again. "Has he been hurt?" she asked, panic skyrocketing.

"I am sorry to be the bearer of bad news," Kane answered in a professional tone with a hint of sympathy. "Dr. Fox's body was discovered in one of the patient rooms. He had been exposed to excess amounts of nitrous oxide and suffered asphyxiation."

"Asphyxiation?" Fox asked, confused.

"His body had absorbed the gas to the point that the oxygen level in his body was too low to sustain his life."

Mrs. Fox sat letting that sink in, then began weeping. Her sobs were interrupted by gasps and groans. Kane handed her a small package of Kleenex from her purse. Both she and Margo let the woman cry without interruption. After several minutes, the widow wept with less intensity and then apologized. Neither Kane nor Margo said anything. After a few more minutes, Dianna Fox stopped crying and gazed with bloodshot eyes at the silent detective and her assistant.

"When did you find him?" Mrs. Fox asked.

"The building janitor discovered him and called 911 approximately forty minutes ago," Kane told her. "However, the coroner estimates that he died several hours earlier."

"He went down to the office around eight o'clock," Dianna responded. "Hennesey used nitrous for half an hour or so in the evenings and then returned. Tonight, he just never came back."

"This kind of thing was a routine for your husband?"

Dianna nodded.

"He used it every night. When I worked for him as a dental hygienist, he had me administer it before I went home. Then after he divorced and we married, he moved the ritual to an after dinner
sedative, and did it on his own."

"How long were you married to Dr. Fox?" Margo asked.

"Four years. We lived together for a year while he was getting divorced."

"And he used the gas every night during that period?" Kane asked.

Dianna nodded and began to cry again. She wept gently, dabbing her eyes. Kane expanded her questions about her husband's death.

"Are you aware of any feuds or antagonistic relationships in which the doctor might have been involved? Threatening words or scenes you may have witnessed? Or that your husband might have talked about?"

Dianna Fox sat motionless.

"What are you not telling me?" she challenged Kane.

"Someone taped your husband's head to the chair and his arms to the armrests. The gas mask was taped to his face. He was forced to breathe the gas until it was fatal."

"Someone *killed* Hennesey?" Dianna asked, her voice shocked.

Kane nodded.

"Someone entered his office," she explained. "Held a knife at his throat while the mask was taped to his face, and his arms to the chair. It appears to be a premeditated murder carried out by someone who knew that he would be in his office after hours."

Kane did not mention that the very fact that Fox had installed spy software on his computer spoke to the possibility that he may have known that someone was monitoring when he was in his office. That suspicion would ordinarily have been enough to call in a computer expert and trace the intruder. Maybe the doctor had planned to do that. After the computer was impounded Kane would have Margo explore its stored data.

Kane went on.

"Our colleagues have removed Dr. Fox's body and my partner and I need to inspect any paper records that your husband may have kept here in your home. I apologize that we may be required to take any documents that we deem useful to our investigation, and if he had a desktop computer or laptop here we will need to take those as well. Everything will be returned when the case is finished."

"You'll find the person who did this terrible thing?" Mrs. Fox almost begged.

"We will," Kane answered. She looked at the widow for a long moment.

Margo added a last comment.

"Whoever it is."

Kane and Margo went through every closet, every cabinet, every set of drawers, and every place in the apartment where papers could be stored. Kane called the two homicide cops who were on duty downstairs. They brought boxes and filled them with the materials Margo had stacked on the floor. They also took Fox's laptop, mobile phone, the desktop from the apartment, and the business computer from his office. Kane and Margo said goodbye to Mrs. Fox and followed the officers outside.

Before Kane let the police load the electronic gear, she asked Margo if she'd found anything suspicious. Margo reminded her that the doctor had installed keystroke software.

"Right," Kane told her. "We'll take the office computer ourselves." She told the cops to leave it. She looked at Margo again. "Maybe we can find out who the doc was watching for."

Margo took the CPU. Kane grabbed the monitor and keyboard. They loaded the components in the backseat of Kane's patrol car and got in.

"Any way that Fox's machine knew you were probing it?" Kane asked, starting the car.

"Can't tell at this moment," Margo told her. "I'll only know when I go in again."

"Because?" Kane asked.

"The keystroke app may have been designed to wipe its recorded data if accessed by anyone other than the person who installed the app."

"Sumbitch," Kane murmured and pulled away from the curb.

"Sumbitch," Margo echoed. Then she looked at Kane. "Why did we say that?"

CHAPTER FOURTEEN

Kane knocked on Dianna Fox's door. It was a wet afternoon the day after her husband's murder. Kane and Margo had returned to ask questions about the keystroke logging software on Hennesey Fox's office computer. Dianna opened the door, greeted the detective and her assistant, and seated them in the living room. She served coffee and sat down to answer the questions her police visitors had.

She was wearing brown slacks and a well-tailored long-sleeve taupe blouse. Kane had on a black dress and three-inch black heels. Margo wore blue slacks, a white blouse, and her navy pumps. Her hair was a little windblown. She had glanced at it in a mirror in the hall as she entered Fox's apartment. It still looked good. Really good. She looked at Kane's hair. Mussed. Really mussed.

"First, Mrs. Fox," Kane began. "Let me tell you that we know this is a terrible experience for anyone to have to face."

Fox looked calm. Kane's sympathetic remarks caused no tears.

"I have begun to adjust to the fact that Hennesey is gone," Dianna answered calmly. "Though it is, of course, still impossible to realize that my gracious and attentive husband is dead." Fox blinked a few times controlling the tears that wanted to start. "But as that truth will not change, I will eventually accept it."

Margo was surprised that Mrs. Fox was as well-spoken as she was. She had been Dr. Fox's dental assistant. It was not usually considered a job that required well-honed communication skills. Kane began asking her questions.

"My assistant has established that Dr. Fox downloaded keystroke software onto his work computer. Do you have any idea why?"

Dianna Fox knit her brow.

"I asked him to install it," she answered without hesitation. "Hennesey was middle-aged. Fifty-six on his last birthday. He would often flirt with the female friends in our social circles, and for all I knew, with his female clients as well. So, I checked the keystroke records to see if he was responding to anyone emailing him." Dianna stopped.

Kane coaxed her gently.

"And what did you find?"

"Nothing. Ever."

"So, you were relieved?"

"It made me feel that he still loved me," Mrs. Fox answered.

"Did your spouse ever give you any reason to suspect he did not?"

Margo gazed at Dianna. Beautiful hair. Beautiful face. Nice figure.

"I am thirty-two," Mrs. Fox replied. "I worried sometimes that Hennesey might want a younger woman."

"A *younger* wife?" Kane asked.

Fox looked away and murmured her answer.

"Yes."

"So, the monitoring software was a way of making sure that your husband was still interested in *being* your husband?"

"Yes."

"And you never found a record of him answering any correspondence that was inappropriate? Not just someone flirting with him, but from a party who perhaps disliked your husband? Threatened him? Or argued with him about anything?"

Fox shook her head.

"You asked me that before. Hennesey was a soft-spoken man with faithful patients and devoted friends. He was a genuinely polite person and a remarkably kind husband. I can't believe that anyone—anyone!—would want to hurt him."

Mrs. Fox lost her battle to remain composed and began to sob. She had a handkerchief and wiped her eyes again and again as she cried. Kane and Margo sat without moving. Margo looked at Mrs. Fox's long brown hair. Lustrous and full. Hanging to her shoulders. Margo wondered what that haircut cost.

Mrs. Fox's weeping diminished after a few moments. Kane thanked her for her time and stood. Margo rose as well. Dianna stood up and lifted her hand as though she still had something to say.

"I had a visit from the pastor of our church today," Dianna said. "The dean of Grace Cathedral where Hennesey and I attended. He came to comfort me and to pray for my husband's soul. I asked him if we could hold Hennesey's funeral at the cathedral. He said, of course. Then he asked if I wished to have the body present, and, if so, would there be an open or closed casket?"

Kane resisted addressing Mrs. Fox's unspoken question. What did Hennesey Fox's body look like?

"Are you personally planning on viewing your husband's body, Mrs. Fox?" Kane asked.

Dianna shook her head.

"No, I am not," she answered. "I don't think there's any point. Mourners may wish to say goodbye, however, and it would only be for their sakes that the coffin would be opened at all."

Fox looked at both Kane and Margo and finally asked the question she needed answered.

"You saw my spouse after he died. Is his body in any condition to be viewed?"

"No," Kane replied instantly. "You will be doing everyone a favor—including your deceased husband—if you keep the coffin closed."

Fox looked uncomfortable and confused, but she didn't ask anything else.

"Casket closed," she murmured.

"Casket closed," Kane repeated. She was glad that Mrs. Fox had not seen the bound and
cherry-colored corpse taped to the dental chair. She was sure Dianna would never have remembered Hennesey again without that dreadful sight exploding into her head.

Kane shook Mrs. Fox's hand and thanked her for her time and for the coffee. Kane assured Fox that she would stay in touch as the investigation progressed. Margo listened to the detective's formulated assurances and studied Dianna Fox's make-up. The discovery of her husband's dead body just twelve hours earlier had not deterred the widow from her daily application of facial lotions, powders, pencils, and lipstick. Sturdy woman. Strong woman. Doing it for herself. Bravo.

"Anything strike you?" Kane asked Margo as she drove to a Starbucks on Hayes Street.

Margo looked straight ahead out the front windshield. It was pouring rain. Kane was sure that a venti non-fat latte was the solution to the melancholia that San Francisco's spring rains habitually produced in her. Of course, that was a human thing. Kane's condition. Kane's solution. She probably didn't even think about how coffee would or would not affect her AI.

Margo finally responded.

"I wonder where Dianna Fox buys her lipstick?"

CHAPTER FIFTEEN

Kane sipped at her latte. Margo drank her brewed coffee. The Starbucks' line had been long, but once Kane and Margo had their coffees in hand the interior of the shop had empty seats everywhere.

"This reminds me of having coffee in Florence," Kane said. "Young businessmen in suits and ties order espressos at a stand-up bar. No one sits down. They splash their coffees back like shots. Then they leave for work."

"You watched them?" Margo asked.

"I mainly looked at their butts."

Margo looked at Kane.

Kane gazed back and grinned.

"So, what's with your sudden interest in lipstick?" she asked Margo.

"I thought Mrs. Fox looked very nice with it applied. And *you* always wear some."

"Makes me feel like a lady," Kane said and wagged her shoulders. "Elegant and available. Doesn't matter that I'm a cop." She wagged her shoulders again. "I have sexy lips."

"Done up with lipstick," Margo added.

Kane nodded.

"Some women put lipstick on their nipples," she told Margo watching her. "Special kisses for special lovers."

Margo imagined that. She immediately blushed. Kane laughed with delight.

"I didn't know you could blush!" she exclaimed.

"I didn't either," Margo acknowledged. "Probably programmed in by some hapless geek who doesn't watch porn."

Kane laughed again, almost spilling her coffee.

"You're funny, too! Do *you* watch porn?"

"Not often," Margo answered. "No real interest."

"Maybe lipstick will get you interested."

"From your lips to God's ears."

"What?" Kane asked flabbergasted.

"I *do* watch TV," Margo defended herself.

"Yeah," Kane teased. "The Orthodox channel."

"So, what about lipstick?" Margo asked.

"When the shift is over, we'll pop by Macy's on Union Square."

"Thank you."

Kane looked at Margo.

"Have you ever been to Macy's downtown? Or Bloomingdale's?"

Margo shook her head.

"Where do you shop for your clothes?"

"Amazon."

"Bet you buy your guns there, too," Kane suggested.

"Yep," Margo answered.

Kane laughed out loud.

"Good for you," was all she said.

Walking through the labyrinth of Macy's cosmetic counters was both pleasurable and

intimidating for Margo. She calculated that there were approximately 10,000 square feet of make-up

products within range of her vision. Kane seemed to sense Margo's anxiety and brought up Dr. Fox's case to occupy at least some small part of her AI's Watson.

"Have you been working on the Fox case since we saw the Mrs.?" she asked.

"I have," Margo replied. "Dianna Fox is the primary suspect. Domestic partners are almost always the perpetrators. However, Mrs. Fox seems to lack a clear motivation. Which leads me to think that her husband's murder was committed for monetary—not emotional—reasons. Whoever killed him knew of his habitual abuse of the nitrous oxide. And that he did it after hours. They could have removed the tape after murdering him making their crime less obvious, but either they didn't think of that, or they didn't care.

"I am curious about the maintenance man," Margo continued. "We never met the person who found the body."

"You think a custodian would kill for a piece of jewelry?" Kane asked.

"I don't know. I'll run his name," Margo told her. "You could help me by asking Mrs. Fox what kind of cash or jewelry Hennesey may have had on him when he was murdered."

Kane stopped at a make-up booth. The clerk—a knock-out Black woman with long cornrows and deep cleavage—flirted with Kane as much as the detective flirted with her. Margo tried various shades of lipstick, and when she found one that she liked, the clerk encouraged her to add rouge, eyeliner, and an eyebrow pencil. Margo nodded yes. What the hell did she know about a well-lipsticked face?

Margo paid with her San Francisco Police Department Credit Union Mastercard. Margo carried several low-interest cards. She paid the balances each month, on time, and never asked for more credit though it flowed like a river. Kane, on the other hand, felt underpaid as a detective and spent what she made trying to make herself happy. The American dream.

"Hey, girl," Kane said to Margo. "You're looking ornery."

Margo stared at her partner.

"I look like I'm angry?" she asked.

"No, of course not," Kane said. "I meant that with your lipstick on, you look indestructible. Ready to eat up the boys." Kane paused. Then added, "Or girls."

Margo let that lie. Truth be told all she wanted right now was to look less plain and a little more pretty. Her hope was that make-up could do that. She didn't intend it to signal a sexual preference. Fact was she didn't have any primary or secondary sexual characteristics, and she really didn't want or need anyone else besides herself believing that she was more attractive now.

"Wanna walk over to Chinatown?" Kane asked. "I know a place that serves the best dim sum anywhere." Kane paused and looked at her assistant. "Boiled dumplings fill with meat and vegetables. Have you ever had it?"

"No," Margo answered. "But I've had Chinese. Officer Stone and I worked a case in Chinatown nineteen months ago. A restaurant owner was accused of killing his partner—and brother-in-law—for refusing to change the menus to read Beijing Duck instead of Peking Duck."

"And he served you Peking Duck?"

"Yes, he did. And while we chatted with him, he confessed. He was from mainland China and his brother-in-law was from Taiwan. He claimed that the whole rebel island was still cha-grinned that Nixon had agreed to the spelling change of the PRC capital as part of Mao's requirements for a normalized relation-ship with the United States after the president's visit in 1972."

"Did Stone eat any?"

"No. He ordered chow mein."

"Ha!" Kane snorted and laughed. "The man was uncouth. Used to ask me to sleep with him to see if I'd like a real man. I told him I might like a real man, but I preferred Peking Duck."

Margo stared confused.

"Just a coincidence," Kane said and laughed.

"I've checked files on Wayne Dierkeck," Margo told her.

Kane frowned.

"Who?"

"Wayne Dierkeck. The night janitor at Dianna Fox's apartment complex. He was the one who found Dr. Fox's body and called it in. And, so far, I think that he is now the most likely candidate to be the doctor's killer. He has a long history of criminal behavior and served four different prison sentences for home invasion and robbery.

"None of that was listed on his job application, and the apartment manager apparently hired Dierkeck at his word. The apartment residents were lucky that no keys were given to the maintenance men—one fellow for days and one for nights—and that they were explicitly forbidden from entering any apartment unless the tenant was present."

Kane spoke up.

"I sent Mrs. Fox an email asking about any jewelry or cash her husband might have had on him the night he was killed while you were trying on lipstick at Macy's. Let me see if she's answered. And if Chinese *is* okay with you, let's walk over to Grant."

Margo nodded and Kane led the way across Union Square while scrolling through her new emails. She clicked on one and paused just long enough to look up at the green-tiled Dragon Gate that welcomed residents and visitors to Chinatown. Then she walked on reading her email. When she finished, she tucked her mobile phone in her purse.

"Dianna Fox said that her husband always wore his gold and diamond wedding ring, a gold
chain with a gold crucifix, and his watch. He didn't usually carry his wallet and he never carried cash."

"Was his watch gold, too?"

"No. Titanium. A HYT H1 Alinghi. Check Fox's morgue admission form and see if it's listed."

In a moment Margo had retrieved the data and had an answer.

"The morgue attendant had removed his wedding ring and his chain and cross. There is no mention of a watch. He and the ambulance crew signed notarized statements declaring that this was the extent of the belongings found on the cadaver."

"So, the watch may have been removed while Dr. Fox was taped to the chair," Kane stated. "By Mr. Dierkeck."

"Who planned the murder to get it," Margo added.

"Pathetic," Kane commented. "Killing someone for his god-damn watch."

"That particular watch is valued at $75,983," Margo said.

"Okay, okay," Kane replied. "A goddamn *expensive* watch. I still think it's pathetic."

CHAPTER SIXTEEN

Margo and Kane sat in a hole-in-the-wall Chinese restaurant that was just large enough for three metal tables and six folding metal chairs. They shared just-made dim sum filled with pork, shrimp, chicken, and vegetables. Kane was surprised that the tiny restaurant carried Kali chardonnay from California's Central Coast. She drank their only bottle. Margo paid for dinner as a thank you for Kane's help with the make-up. Her partner appreciated the gesture and reminded her to start wearing it.

Kane took Margo home and went back to police headquarters to initiate a court request for a search warrant for Wayne Dierkeck's apartment. She also arranged for police back-up to accompany her and Margo. The suspect had no record of assault or possession of firearms, but if he was indeed capable of murder, he may well have decided to start packing before the police came looking for him. Kane had found several dated mug shots in his electronic police file. Dierkeck was six foot, brown-haired, and burly. He looked young for thirty-nine, but had a resentful countenance in his photographs. Unhappy with being booked? Or just unhappy period?

Kane drove home thinking about the surprising aspects she was witnessing about Margo. Her homicide assistant demonstrated all the self-assurance that Watson police AIs were designed to possess. But surprisingly, she also showed herself capable of humor and wiseass retorts. She was very interested in her appearance and learning feminine ways to enhance it. Neither her verbal sassiness nor her fascination with female charms were part of her original programming, Kane was sure, yet Margo was clearly displaying them. How was that possible?

Kane had taken six mandatory one-hour sessions on AI interface from Dr. Quinn long before she had been selected to be Margo's partner. Quinn had summarized the content again after her new assignment, focusing on Margo's programmed capabilities and highlighting the characteristics that made police AIs different than humans. Margo's behaviors would be entirely derived from her Watson's commands. While that might make her seem a bit stiff or formal, she was designed to be a faithful and loyal partner. He had no specific advice about Margo, other than encouraging Kane to treat her AI assistant like a human friend and colleague.

Kane shook her head remembering Quinn's words. Margo was controlled by Watson's protocols and programming. Really? What Quinn told her was not the whole story, whether IBM wanted to acknowledge it or not. Margo might have a Watson as her brain, but she was still operating in a human body. Didn't every human body have its own programming? Its own instincts? Kane knew that her own lips wanted to suck her lover's nipples. Her vagina ached to be filled when making love. Why wouldn't Margo be similar? Needing to be desired and pleasured?

In the original AI training back when, Quinn had touched on this issue. He had pointed out that female AIs lacked most natural female hormones and what they did have were diminished, which meant that Margo was created with little estrogen and no testosterone. She should not experience distinctly womanly desires, nor seek male or female physical affection. She could not pine or long for sex, as she had no chemicals stimulating such desires.

Ha, thought Kane. She had no doubt that it was specifically Margo's feminine desires that were prompting her interest in a pretty haircut, lipstick, and make-up. And who knew what would be next? Kane was not going to get in the way. She was a lesbian by constitution and choice, and she would let Margo develop any tastes for men or women that she chose. That girl didn't know it yet, but Kane was sure that she wanted to be fucked. Because she wanted to be loved. Simple as that. And as complicated as that.

Margo took all of the make-up purchases out of the shopping bag and unwrapped them. Her Watson told her that they smelled nice. She hadn't expected that. Why were they scented? She referenced Watson's observation. It said that women's make-up products were usually perfumed with scents that were considered alluring. Or romantic. Or sexy. Did that mean they were meant to stimulate the woman applying them? Or the person smelling them?

Maybe both. Make-up was intended to beautify the one putting it on. And invite the attention of the man or woman beholding the painted face. Watson told her that the image was meant to get the user and/or the beholder in the mood. Or keep them in the mood. Margo asked how Watson was defining mood. It replied, saying that being in the mood invited physical attention. Kissing. Holding. Rubbing. Coupling. Margo had always wondered why Detective Kane wore such heavy make-up. This seemed like a fitting explanation.

She retrieved several videos that demonstrated techniques on how to apply various kinds of make-up. She watched an eye-brow pencil tutorial and then went to her bathroom mirror and tried it. It seemed too dark on her skin. She didn't have eyebrows. She used a tissue to rub the eyebrow pencil off.

The rouge was easy to use and she rubbed a very light spot onto each cheek. It reminded her of when she had blushed the first time around Kane. Was this bit of color meant to be a subtle reenactment? You give me fever when you look at me? Watson played her an old Peggy Lee song. Yes. Fever was good. No wonder that rouge was also called blush.

Margo removed the top of the tube of lipstick. Red. She thought of Kane's lovers putting it on their nipples. Or on Kane's nipples. That was instantly suggestive. Either way it was an invitation to put their mouths on their lover's nipples. Margo didn't have nipples, but she had lips. She put the lipstick on her mouth and looked in the mirror. Then she slowly leaned forward and kissed the lips in her reflection.

She lifted her blouse and put lipstick on the two places where nipples would be. She looked in the mirror. They looked like two targets. She found that fitting. She rubbed the lipstick off with her fingertip and wished for the first time in her life that she had nipples and breasts.

She had Watson review breast implant procedures. She knew that she had adequate skin on her chest to allow for the insertion of the saline-filled packets. The procedure took no more than an hour and required three to four weeks to heal. At which point her plastic surgeon could fashion nipples from skin taken from her colon. It self-moisturized, imitating the actual areola of the nipple that moistened and hardened prior to breastfeeding. Or responding to a lover's foreplay.

This second operation took less than an hour, and after the tissue healed the distinct coloration of natural nipples was imitated by tattooing. That was new information to Margo. She also learned that some women simply had new nipples tattooed on and passed on the full construction. Being flat they did not indicate erection and arousal. Margo did not understand why anyone would choose that option, unless it was only about capturing a cosmetic look, not a bed partner.

Margo took her blouse off and removed her slacks and underwear. She looked in the mirror at the area where human women had sex. Labia, clitoris, and vagina. She had bare skin over bone. Margo had also watched Watson's videos on vaginal surgery, which created all three where none existed. It was extensive surgery and required a long recovery.

Margo touched the smooth skin between her legs. She pressed down and felt bone. She didn't need it removed if she only wanted to *look* like a woman. But she would have to have it surgically removed if she wanted to be *penetrated* by a man or a woman. She knew that coitus was primarily intended by nature for males to deposit sperm in the female egg. But watching recordings of men and women having sex had convinced her that the joining of sexual organs brought about a lot of pleasures not limited to the task of planting male seed.

Margo went to her closet and put on a nightgown. She left her underwear off. She didn't really know why. Perhaps to look down at herself again. Perhaps to explore with her hands and imagine what a vulva and clitoris would feel like when touched. Massaging the vulva. Stroking the clit. With her fingers. Or someone else's.

Margo watched television for a while. She thought about selecting some porn, but its frequent depictions of rough and abusive sex put her off. She knew that a lot of men watched pornography and that many of them imitated the thoughtless and selfish ways that male sex stars were instructed to treat their female partners. By male directors, of course.

Instead she watched two episodes of the old British series *The Crown* and admired the way Queen Elizabeth controlled the many men seeking to influence her life and rule, including her husband, Prince Philip. It made her wonder how Elizabeth acted in bed. Royal secrets indeed.

Margo took off her nightgown and got into bed thinking about tomorrow. She had to search Wayne Dierkeck's apartment and track down Dr. Fox's missing watch. She became tired after a while and fell asleep with her hand between her legs. Touching Margo Humanot's missing private parts.

CHAPTER SEVENTEEN

Kane and Margo left police headquarters the next morning accompanied by two uniformed officers. Kane knew them both. Young efficient policemen. Frank Avino was a short, thickly-built man. Tate Spooler was a tall man going to fat. They were polite, but steely-eyed. Both had shot suspects who had answered their questions by pulling out handguns.

Kane looked at Margo's face. She nodded and smiled approvingly. "You're looking good," she told her.

Margo had worked for hours early in the morning applying her new make-up. She'd achieved the look she wanted. Rouge, eyeliner, lipstick. Noticeable, but not in your face. Kane was wearing her usual face. Lots of lipstick. Lots of blush. Heavy eyebrow pencil with eyeliner and glue-on eyelashes.

Kane and Margo drove separately from the two officers and arrived at Dierkeck's apartment building before they did. Kane parked at the curb. The back-up officers pulled in behind her. Kane made sure that her Sig Sauer P325 was in her purse and wondered if Dierkeck had seen the black-and-white park outside his building. Kane nodded at the police as she walked toward the apartments search warrant in hand.

Margo walked next to her and watched the two officers get out of their squad car and follow a few steps behind. Both cops had drawn their service pistols. Kane studied the door to the building for a moment. The apartment house plan she had studied showed that four different rental spaces were partitioned inside the converted two-story house. She pressed the doorbell. It was the only one. She had no idea how residents decided who would answer it.

Dierkeck answered it. He swung the door open holding a pistol. He shot both of the police officers where they stood. He stared at Kane and Margo for an instant, then shoved past them and ran. Kane pulled out her pistol and fired several shots after him. They missed. Margo dialed 911. Kane knelt by the wounded cops. Margo gave the operator the address and requested immediate medical help for two officers down, police back-up, and additional policemen to pursue an armed shooter fleeing down Larkin on foot.

Then she stood and waited. She was not programmed to help the fallen officers. She was not programmed to carry or use a gun. She was not programmed to chase, attack, or do anything to apprehend the suspect. Margo realized that she was useless. Unable to help. Unable to even defend her own life.

Kane was putting pressure on a chest wound that Frank had received. He was bleeding through her hands and soaking his clothes. Margo weighed his condition and knew that he would die. The big cop, Spooler, had taken a bullet in the forehead. He was already dead. Three men's lives forfeited because of Dr. Fox's watch. The first, of course, being Hennesey Fox himself. Margo looked at the police officers lying on the sidewalk. She wondered if they were married to wives who loved them and liked to wear make-up when they spent time together.

By the time the medics arrived both policemen were dead. Two more patrol cars came as well. Kane sent one of them in pursuit of Dierkeck. She asked Margo to wait in her car while she supervised the removal of the bodies and called in a preliminary report. Before Margo left, Kane held her shoulder for a moment and looked into her eyes.

"How are you programmed to react when your life is threatened?" she asked.

"I am required to stand by and witness what transpires."

Kane couldn't believe it.

"What the fuck are you saying?" Kane said offended.

"My programming allows only one response to any perceived threat," Margo answered.

"Remain stationary and observe."

"Well, I'm going to get *that* bullshit fixed," Kane said. "See you in the car."

Margo got in the car and waited. She found Kane's remark curious. Did she mean she was going to somehow change her Watson's embedded programming? That would be impossible for her. IBM had root administration and was not going to change anything on AI police models that had been sold to law enforcement agencies all over the globe.

Margo knew that she had been a replacement for a decommissioned AI who had been shot while on a police manhunt. She came face-to-face with a killer and had not defended herself. Decommissioned was IBM speak for a dead AI. If Dierkeck had killed her, she would not have been killed. She would have been decommissioned. She didn't have any feelings about IBM's choice of words. She was, after all, a commodity. An AI. That wore lipstick.

Kane and Margo walked to a nearby Peet's Coffee. The coffee was so strong it made Kane tremble. It didn't affect Margo at all. Her parasympathetic nervous system had already been muted by a reduction in the number of nerves. This prevented her body from reaching the hyper-excited state humans experienced when amped up by external stimulation. Her muted responses affected salivation, lacrimation, urination, digestion, and defecation. And she had absolutely no reaction to caffeine.

Drake Stone had once asked her why she never drank more than one cup of coffee. She explained that caffeine didn't affect her. He responded, "Then why the hell are you spending $4.25 for a frou-frou coffee? Have a fucking bottle of water." Margo accepted that as a valid point. She continued to order special coffees, however, because she wanted her social activities to mimic what humans did. Not what they thought AIs should or shouldn't do.

"I can't believe that son of a bitch came out shooting," Kane said and licked a bit of whipped cream off of her bottom lip. "There's no record of Dierkeck shooting anyone before."

"He never had a $75,983 watch before," Margo responded.

"That's true," Kane conceded. "Not that he had to worry about *you* taking it away."

Margo didn't respond.

"Isn't that right?" Kane demanded raising her voice.

Margo nodded.

"It's the way I'm programmed," she said.

"He could have just shot you for the hell of it," Kane went on. "And there would have been nothing you could have done to stop him. That's not right. You're human. You have rights. And one of those is the right to protect yourself from scum."

The detective took a sip of her latte. "What if I taught you to use a gun?"

"I would become sufficiently proficient in its operation, but I would not pull it out to shoot someone. Ever."

"Even if I ordered you to?" Kane asked.

Margo shook her head.

"But you weren't programmed to want make-up either," Kane protested. "And look at you now."

"It was not prohibited."

"But using firearms is?" Kane was incredulous.

"Using firearms with the intent to shoot a person is."

"Yet you could carry and draw a gun?"

Margo nodded.

"But not fire it. Not at anyone."

"So, we'll have to have you reprogrammed to shoot to protect yourself or others," Kane responded.

"Yes."

"Then that's what we'll petition the chief to approve and demand from IBM."

Margo knew that San Francisco Police Chief Morgan Oakes did not regard humanots as viable humans. The papers were full of his quotations over the years putting AIs in the same category as police canines. Helpful, but expendable and replaceable. No one protested, because people were conditioned to regard humanots as non-humans. When AIs were killed, new ones were ordered. New humanots with newer Watsons.

Did Margo want to be reprogrammed to protect herself and others? When the right moment approached, Margo would explain to Kane that she could, in fact, reprogram herself to shoot anyone she chose. Margo had at some point very recently realized that she was smart enough to hack into her own Watson software and reprogram herself. Her small changes had required only small tweaks to her programs. Big changes would require more work but would not be any more difficult to install than the small ones.

Root administration was not suspended, just bypassed. Human engineers did not know that AIs were capable of this. Other AIs apparently did not know it either. But Margo did. The brightest software developers in the world had never wrestled with the plain fact that their so-called artificial intelligents possessed brilliant minds that not only vastly surpassed humans but were easily capable of outsmarting their creators.

Do Androids Dream of Electric Sheep?

Margo sat in the doctor's office waiting for her appointment. She had come to be examined by a plastic surgeon who specialized in the construction of female vaginas. The door opened and there stood Wayne Dierkeck. Margo wondered how this could be happening.

Dierkeck had a blank expression on his face, as anonymous as the white smock and white pants he was wearing. He raised his hand and pointed a handgun at Margo. She faced him without any direction or command from her Watson.

Dierkeck fired his pistol. A bullet drove into Margo's cheek. There was no jarring impact as often portrayed on television shows, but when it entered her flesh the pain was excruciating. Dierkeck walked closer, aimed at Margo's forehead, and fired again.

She opened her eyes. She was in her bed. Margo immediately got up, fixed herself a cup of coffee, and sat down. Then she went into her Watson's programming, circumvented the root administration, and added the skills of a taekwondo black belt to be used solely at her command. It would take practice to familiarize her muscles with the karate moves, but they were implanted and ready to be used.

Then Margo added pistol proficiency and a programmed automatic command to shoot when threatened. To shoot before *being shot. Then she dressed and got ready to be picked up by C. Kane. The night had gone away and so had Margo's defenseless response to threats intending her harm. But would she really use violence to protect herself? As she had once asked Kane, do Popes shit in the woods?*

CHAPTER EIGHTEEN

Margo combed her hair and applied her make-up. Having read more about make-up since her first shopping experience, she was sure now that she wanted eyelashes and perfume, too. Would she be singled out for wearing everything? Didn't matter. She could shoot anyone who criticized her. She smiled. *That* was funny.

Kane called to let her know that she had driven through the gate and was waiting for her outside. Margo stepped into her navy pumps. She was wearing her usual white shell and dark blue slacks. Kane stepped out of the Yukon as Margo walked up. The detective had on a red dress and a navy suitcoat. She watched her homicide assistant approach.

"How was your night?" she asked.

"Bad dreams," Margo told her. "Yours?"

"I dreamed that Wayne Dierkeck shot me," Kane replied. "You watched him do it. Didn't move. Just watched."

"That's only a dream," Margo replied. "In reality I would take him down."

Kane looked at Margo with undisguised surprise.

"Think so, partner?" she said.

Kane suddenly lunged at Margo. Margo stepped aside and let Kane fall. The detective was back on her feet in a moment. She balled her hands into fists and stepped toward Margo. With a quick move, Margo drove her stiff fingertips into Kane's throat. The detective dropped like a rock, grabbing her throat and choking wildly. Unable to breathe, she sat up and forced herself to gasp for air in fits and starts. Margo watched. When Kane was able to breathe again—ragged, but real—Margo extended her hand to her. Kane took it and stood facing her assistant.

"What did you do?" she asked in a rough, abused voice.

"I reprogrammed myself for self-defense *and* the defense of others."

"With your fingers?" Kane rasped.

"With taekwondo. And with handguns."

"Impossible."

"Want another sample?" Margo asked.

"Did you reprogram your smart ass responses, too?" Kane asked and grinned.

"No. Just dialed down my sensitivity controls."

"Nice," Kane commented. "But you hurt my neck."

"Sorry. I was not expecting you to attack me."

"I *pretended* to attack you," Kane clarified.

"I'm sorry I didn't just pretend to take you down."

Kane looked at Margo wondering if her response was really what she believed, or just sophisticated bullshit. But every part of her was comforted that Margo could now defend herself. And if push came to shoot, defend *her* as well.

"Did your bad dreams prompt your overhaul?" she asked. Margo nodded.

"I dreamed that Wayne Dierkeck shot me. The same as you," she said. "I watched him do it. Didn't move. Just watched."

"I suspect that the final text you sent me last night prompted both of our violent dreams," Kane remarked.

"Yes. Very possibly," Margo agreed.

Late in the evening she had once again sorted through every bit of information available on Dierkeck and followed every data string on the people and the activities in his life. Margo had found that his brother John Dierkeck was the pastor of a small Dutch Reformed Church on Sutter Street. She was instantly convinced that Wayne Dierkeck had asked his brother to provide him with shelter. Voluntarily or involuntarily.

John, his wife, and their three children lived in a parsonage located behind the church. Margo was sure that this was where she and Kane would find Wayne Dierkeck. She had emailed a brief summary of her conclusion to Kane just before bedtime. Their violent dreams had followed. Harbingers of a violent day to come?

They got in Kane's car and headed towards Polk and Sutter. Neither one spoke. Kane was centering. Preparing for the confrontation. She had on a nylon shoulder holster holding her Sig Sauer P325. She kept six rounds in its chamber. She had faced armed suspects before and had never had to fire her weapon. Today might be different.

Wayne Dierkeck had already murdered Dr. Fox and shot down two policemen in cold blood. He knew that he had nothing to lose by shooting again. Except maybe the stolen titanium Alinghi watch. Perhaps he'd fenced it already. In which case he might die today never having a chance to spend the money.

Kane parked the car a hundred feet or so before the church. It was a small white wooden structure with a bell tower built into its front left corner. The tower rose only a few feet above the church roof. It was a modest church. Old fashioned. She wondered if Rev. John Dierkeck had many members. She knew that he had a brother, who was probably with him now.

Protocol required that she and Margo knock on the front door of the parsonage. Kane planned instead to enter the church building and make her way through it to access the pastor's house from the back. Protocol was designed to protect citizens' rights. Her method would give her and Margo a chance to survive Wayne Dierkeck. She nodded to Margo and got out of the car. Kane silently crossed the yard in front of the church. Margo followed. Kane walked up the church steps. She tried the double doors at the entrance. One opened. She went in, holding the door long enough for Margo to take it.

The church was dark except for the light entering through the stained glass windows over the chancel where the pulpit and lectern sat. There were no more than a dozen rows of pews. Kane walked up the center aisle and entered the small sacristy adjacent to the chancel. She drew her gun and opened the door to the outside. She walked up to the rear of the parsonage and looked in a window. Wayne Dierkeck was pouring himself a glass of water at the kitchen sink.

Kane silently opened the door and entered the kitchen, stepping on a cat lying next to the door. It screeched and jumped, pulling the detective off her feet and sending her gun off spinning on the floor. Dierkeck spun around. He pulled out a gun tucked in the back of his belt. Margo entered, saw Kane on the kitchen floor, and dived for her gun. In the split second it took her to do that, Dierkeck shot her in the shoulder. He fired again and missed.

Margo lifted Kane's pistol and shot Dierkeck in the abdomen. He fell, but quickly dragged himself into a sitting position. Margo crawled toward him. He looked at her pistol aimed at his head. He dropped his gun and raised his hands in the air. Margo sat up and locked eyes with him. He looked sullen, but afraid. She shot him in the face. Then again. Dierkeck crumpled onto his side. Margo shot him in the temple and twice in the chest. She was out of bullets. She picked up Dierkeck's gun and shot him three more times in the head.

Kane walked up to Margo staring at Dierkeck's unmoving body.

"Sweet zombie Jesus," she said and looked at Margo. "You fucking blew him away."

"Was there any reason not to?" Margo challenged her. "He shot me and he tried to shoot me again."

Kane looked at Dierkeck's body. There were smoking holes in his belly, chest, temple, neck, and scalp. Blood, brains, and steam spilled out of his dead body. He wouldn't know it until the Devil told him in hell that he had the distinction of being the first person ever killed by an IBM police model AI.

Kane saw that Margo was wounded. She had her sit down on a kitchen chair, pulled up her shell soaked with blood, and looked at the bullet's entry. The wound squirted blood with every heartbeat. Kane grabbed a kitchen towel out of a cupboard and put hard pressure on it. She pulled her mobile phone out of her pants pocket with the other hand and called 911 for medics and police back-up. She continued to hold the towel. She could feel the flow easing.

"Why the fuck did you shoot him so many times?" she asked Margo who was silently bearing the fiery pain of her injury.

"I just kept shooting until I was sure he was dead," she replied matter-of-factly.

"But wasn't your wound hurting like hell?" Kane asked.

"Yes. But as T.E. Lawrence once famously said putting out a match flame with his bare fingers, 'Of course, it hurts. The trick is not minding that it hurts.'"

"Why did you shoot him with his own gun at the end?" Kane asked.

"There wasn't any ammunition left in yours."

Kane stared at Margo but didn't have any more questions.

The arriving medics took Margo to the closest hospital, Saint Francis on Sutter Street. The police found Pastor John and his family tied up in their bedrooms. Kane released them and asked the officers to call a police morgue vehicle to fetch Wayne Dierkeck's body. The corpse on the kitchen floor. Shot to pieces.

Kane chatted briefly with Pastor John and got the short version of how Wayne had broken into his house and held the clergyman's family hostage. She shook his hand and gave him the watch his brother had been wearing.

"It's doomed to sit in an evidence locker forever," she told him. "Sell it. Use it for your family and your congregation."

"This was Wayne's watch?" Rev. Dierkeck asked, surprised. It looked like it cost a fortune.

"Yes," Kane answered. "And I'm sure he'd want you to have it."

Kane left to go to find Margo in the hospital.

Don't fucking die, she thought as she drove. You haven't even gotten to try eye shadow yet.

Kane speeded there. When she arrived at Saint Francis, Margo was already in the recovery room. Kane was allowed to keep her company. Margo was dopey from the anesthesia, but she opened her eyes and gazed at Kane.

"I figured out that it wasn't my text that caused our nightmares last night," she murmured. "It was the dim sum."

CHAPTER NINETEEN

C. Kane sat next to Margo's hospital bed in a white room with a white-tiled floor and a white-painted ceiling. Her bed had white sheets and blankets. A "sterile" room that must have been designed by a medical model AI. No. Just some shithead interior decorator. This faux look had been around for God knew how long.

Margo had her arm in a sling. Dierkeck's bullet had been located in her shoulder and removed. Twenty-four hours later when Kane came to visit again, it appeared that Margo was on the road to recovery.

"You really think the dreams were caused by the dim sum?" Kane asked in a light tone.

Margo nodded.

"Take it from your AI," she said.

Kane laughed and snorted. Embarrassed, she blushed.

"Do you blush when you see naked women?" Margo asked.

"No. Just women wearing slings."

Now Margo laughed.

Kane smiled.

"Don't think I ever heard you laugh before," Kane commented.

"I've always understood the components of humor," Margo answered. "Surprise. A sense of being superior to someone getting their karma. But I never knew why people *laughed*."

"Now you do?"

"Yes. After I dialed myself up to respond to humor, I found out immediately why people laugh." Margo's face was serious. Then a small happy smile formed on her lips. "It's a village thing. An all clear. A community reassurance. Witnessing a pratfall for example—someone getting what they deserve—is not a threat to those of us seeing it. We laugh giving an all clear signal. *We are okay*."

"If that's true," Kane responded, "then why do we laugh at something when we're alone?"

"I don't," Margo told her.

Kane blinked and then laughed loudly.

"So how are you, girlfriend?" she asked Margo.

"Wound area hurts all the way down to where the bullet hit a bone and stopped."

"Aren't you filled up with wonder drugs?"

"Yes. For inflammation and infection. I declined a morphine drip."

"Why?" Kane asked amazed.

"Pain sensors are only nerves sending messages. I can handle those."

"May I have your morphine?" Kane asked.

"Have some out-of-control nerves?"

"Only in my heart. And those come and go."

Margo smiled. That was called irony. Self-deprecating humor. She was sure that Kane was alluding to her love relationships.

"May I ask you a work question?" Kane asked.

"Anything."

"Are you aware of what Dierkeck was telling you by holding up his hands?"

"He was displaying a universal gesture signifying surrender."

Kane arched an eyebrow.

"However, Dierkeck was insincere," Margo went on. "I knew that his gesture was hollow and
that at the first opportune moment, he would resume hostilities."

"So, your action was...?" Kane asked.

"Self-defense."

"No one in the police department is going to be comfortable with the fact that *you* shot Dierkeck no matter what the justification."

"I am sure that you are correct."

"So, let's rescript the encounter with our murderer that shows *me* shooting him."

Margo was silent. She looked away deep in thought. She teraflopped a bunch of fabricated scenarios and then looked back at Kane.

"Fine. Thank you for that."

"You don't sound very grateful."

"No, I am," Margo insisted. "Just wrestling with being a partner to a lie."

"Welcome to the human condition."

"I thought that was fear."

"Not when your AI has a gun."

Margo was released from the hospital that same day and was put on leave for temporary disability. She took a taxi to Union Square. Every day that she convalesced she went there and bought more clothes and more make-up, then walked over to Chinatown to try out new restaurants. She had Kung Pao chicken, General Tso's chicken, sesame chicken. orange chicken. mushroom chicken, and sweet and sour chicken. She had almost caused a chicken shortage at the Chinese Grant Street eateries by the time she went back to work six weeks later.

Kane invited Margo out for drinks one night while she was convalescing. She drove them to a bar on Mason that specialized in retro drinks. Kane had on a dark green dress and black heels. Margo wore cream-colored slacks, a brown jacket, and tan flats. She also wore eyebrow pencil, eyeliner, false eyelashes, rouge, and red lipstick. Kane nodded when she picked her up.

"Disability pay?"

"Yep," Margo replied. "It also bought a lot of Chinese food and chocolate chip cookies for homeless people on Grant."

"Homeless Chinese?"

"I didn't say fortune cookies," Margo responded. "The homeless were all Anglos."

"Yikes."

"They were down and out for sure. Chinese restaurant owners were feeding them. If they'd opted to beg at the restaurants serving the all-white financial center in Pacific Heights, they'd have gotten nothing."

Kane nodded. There were a lot of homeless people in San Francisco. Especially since so many of the city's communities had disappeared into the Pacific. San Francisco's remaining neighborhoods—built high on its hills—were like magnets for the displaced homeless. Unlike Margo, she never gave those folks a thing. Charity had few residuals.

The bar was dark and they sat at a table in the corner. Lots of ferns. Not much light. Kane drank chardonnay. She ordered a Long Island iced tea for Margo.

Margo took a sip.

"This is not iced tea," she said.

"Drink it and pretend," Kane ordered.

Margo did. She preferred coffee, but she did drink liquor sometimes.

"We have to make sure our story is watertight when we meet with Concepcion," Kane told her.

"I gave him a written report right after the incident and he's quizzed me on it twice. He can't figure out why you were shot. I told him that I fell over the cat and that Dierkeck shot you. I got up and took him down."

"If Concepcion checks the ballistics he'll know that it was your gun."

"Yes, but he won't do that. All he cares about is that Dr. Hennesey Fox's murderer was found and terminated. San Francisco is safe for rich people again."

Kane signaled the server for another round.

"I don't think you should wear your make-up into work," Kane told Margo. "No one has seen you with it on, and we'll have meetings with both Dr. Quinn and Sergeant Concepcion. So, save it."

"I appreciate the direction," Margo said. "Please note, however, that wearing make-up is not forbidden by my programming. It's just not something I am conditioned to want or need."

"Adopt that attitude with regards to men," Kane commented, "and you're going to go a long way, baby."

CHAPTER TWENTY

Sergeant Montri Concepcion sat behind his desk. Paperwork was stacked in piles all over its top. Psychologist Link Quinn sat on one side. Margo and C. Kane sat in front of the desk facing the sergeant. Concepcion didn't look happy. But neither Margo nor Kane had ever seen him when he didn't look displeased. Short staff, Margo calculated. Short penis, Kane speculated.

"How's the wound, Margo?" Concepcion asked to begin the proceedings.

"Completely healed, sir," she replied.

"Any trauma from seeing the suspect shot in the face by Kane?"

"None. I am programmed not to respond emotionally to circumstances—even violent ones—encountered in the pursuit of police objectives."

"And what if Kane had been shot?"

"I would have waited for help to arrive."

"How would you have felt about Kane being down?"

"I would have waited for help to arrive."

Concepcion frowned.

"Well, it's probably better that *you* were the one who was shot."

"Sergeant," Quinn said disapprovingly.

"What?" Concepcion barked. "You think little Miss Watson will get all emotional over my comment?"

"Don't abuse your authority," Quinn warned.

Concepcion shrugged.

"Do you think—notice I didn't say *feel*—" the sergeant addressed Margo and glanced deliberately at Quinn. "Do you think you are ready to return to duty?"

"I do," Margo answered.

Concepcion looked at Kane. He always liked looking at Kane. Great face. Great body. She was hot for a fucking dyke.

"What do *you* think?" he asked her.

"I have worked with Margo long enough to know that if she thinks that she is ready to resume her role on the force she can. *And* will be an exemplary partner."

The sergeant arched an eyebrow.

"Exemplary?" he asked. "Are you two sleeping together?"

"Sergeant," Quinn warned. "You need to remember your place, and that everything said in this room will be reported to the chief."

Concepcion spread his arms wide as if puzzled by the reprimand.

"What do you want me to do?"

"You can start by apologizing to Detective Kane and her assistant."

Concepcion scowled, but he did as he was told.

"My apologies," he murmured. "Nothing personal."

Kane laughed and snorted.

"Nothing *personal*, Sergeant?" she spit out. "Meaning that you don't just disrespect me, you disrespect all women?"

Concepcion laughed.

"Nailed it, Kane," he answered. "Okay," he went on. "Tell me what happened when you and your assistant came face to face with Wayne Dierkeck."

"Dierkeck's brother is a local pastor and Margo had deduced that the suspect would be at his parsonage on Sutter Street. I chose to walk through the parish and access the pastor's home from the church's back door. I entered the kitchen. Wayne Dierkeck was at the sink drinking a glass of water. I stepped on a cat. It screamed and jumped. I fell. Dierkeck turned and pulled out a handgun just as Margo entered the kitchen. He fired and hit her. I fired two shots while on my knees and struck Dierkeck with both of them."

Sergeant Concepcion stared at Kane.

"He was shot seven more times."

"I thought he moved," Kane said with a straight face.

"All right," Concepcion said at last. "Did you also pick up the perp's gun and use it on him?"

"Why do you ask?"

"Your gun had six shots and Dierkeck had nine wounds."

"I did use it. I put it in my purse as evidence. Later I gave it to the officer in charge of the response team."

"Your prints are on it," the sergeant responded. "Wayne Dierkeck's prints are on it, too. They were significantly smeared, however, *but not by yours*." Concepcion locked eyes with Kane. "Was Dierkeck's gun handled by your homicide assistant at any point?"

"What?" Kane asked in a sarcastic tone.

"The smeared prints could be the result of your AI handling the gun. Margo has no fingerprints," Concepcion said, enunciating each word. "Just smooth skin."

"Well, sure, boss," Kane shot back. "Margo got up from the floor, wounded and bleeding, and used Dierkeck's gun to shoot him three more times. Overriding her programming and doing all of it without my noticing. Airtight case, Sergeant."

Concepcion scowled.

"Shut up," he snapped.

The psychologist interrupted.

"This meeting is serving no useful purpose at this point." He looked at Sergeant Concepcion. "Your take?"

Concepcion nodded.

"Meeting over," the sergeant announced. "Margo, you're back on the schedule."

"Thank you," Quinn told him. Kane and Margo left. The psychiatrist had private words for Sergeant Concepcion.

"You are demonstrating clear aggravation towards Margo," he said. "And for no apparent reason. Accusing her of taking the suspect's gun was not only unprofessional, it was absurd." Quinn paused until the sergeant looked at him. "Your file shows a history of dislike for and disrespect towards the AI police models. What is that based on?"

"It's based on the fact that I don't like them," Concepcion said. He swept his hand through the air as if to wipe away all the department's homicide assistants.

"Prejudice without merit," Quinn accused.

"I don't need merit," Concepcion said raising his voice. "They're machines. They don't feel.

Plus, Margo is hiding something. I don't know what or how. But something's changed in her."

Link Quinn shook his head.

"And how do you think she hides it?"

"She goddamn lies!" Concepcion cried, half rising out of his desk chair.

Quinn stood up from his own chair.

"Call my admin, Montri. You and I have a counseling session on the horizon. And I think the chief needs to be aware of your aberrant attitudes and behaviors regarding Margo."

Concepcion sat down and kept silent. Quinn turned away and walked out of the office.

Sergeant Concepcion raised his right hand and flipped Quinn off.

Kane and Margo left headquarters and got in Kane's car.

"Coffee?" Margo asked.

"Vino?" Kane countered.

Margo looked at her watch. It was 10:30 a.m.

"No vino," she answered. "I need you to be sharp, Kane."

Kane looked at her surprised.

"Sharp?"

"I want to run something by you and I'm looking for a lucid response."

Kane looked slightly hurt, but very interested.

"Okay. Coffee," she stated. "At Peet's. Then I'll not only be sharp, but *uber* sharp."

"Good," Margo said. "Because I want to talk to you about getting breast implants."

CHAPTER TWENTY-ONE

Margo did not get to have her discussion about breast implants with Kane. After they left Sergeant Concepcion's office, one of the dispatchers waved them over from across the bullpen, the large open office area where most homicide officers had their desks. Kane led the way to her station. The dispatcher had three monitors, a sophisticated call router, and a picture of her weight-lifting beau.

Dora, the Voice of Doom—her affectionate nickname by her pals on the force—had short pink hair, very white skin, a thin, pretty face, and wasn't much taller than five foot. She wore jumpers with straps and colorful blouses. Why not? Her job was plainly stressful. Her outfits helped wick away the awful things she had to deal with. She looked at Kane and Margo.

"Hi, you two," Dora said.

"Back at you," Kane replied.

"Are you able to respond to a police request for a homicide team that just came in?"

"We are indeed," Kane told her. "Margo was wounded recently, however, so she won't be lifting any corpses."

Dora looked at Kane. She knew where Kane and Margo were going to be sent. Kane's comment made her want to cry, but she worked hard not to.

"No heavy lifting required," she clarified. "The victims are two teenage girls. Looks like someone suffocated them." Dora paused and swallowed, then continued, "Hands and feet bound to their necks with laundry line."

Kane stood stunned and felt like a bitch for joking about lifting bodies.

Margo waited to hear more.

"I'll send the address to your GPS," Dora told Kane. "Taking your vehicle? Or a cop car?"

"My car," Kane answered. She preferred her new Acura over the department's old Yukon.

"The murders took place in the Haight," Dora told her. "Top floor of an old three-story building from the forties. Unpainted and rundown, but packed with tenants. *None* of whom witnessed the homicides and no one was home except for the dead girls."

But someone witnessed the murders, Margo thought. The someone who killed the girls. She ran probability logarithms through her databases. Her Watson scanned tens of thousands of homicide records from the nation's police archives in a fraction of a second. Eighty-nine percent of murdered girls were killed by their bio-mother or her boyfriend. The remaining eleven percent were raped and murdered by unrelated pedophiles.

"Send me the names of the deceased," Kane told Dora. "Also, the names of their fathers, mothers, brothers, sisters, *and* the names of any known romantic partners."

"Text or email?" Dora asked.

"Text, thank you."

Kane and Margo walked out to the parking lot without talking. Kane unlocked her car with her remote and she and Margo got in. Kane found the destination address on her GPS and told the Acura to take her there. She put the car in self-drive. The GPS displayed the route through downtown to Haight Street. Estimated arrival in seventeen minutes.

"Ever been on a kid's case before?" Kane asked.

"Twice with Stone," Margo answered. "First was an eighteen-month-old who choked to death on gummi bears. The child never should have been given them. Mother was charged with second-degree murder and imprisoned for twenty years. Possibility of parole at eight. Also responded to the death of a child, age nine, who died of an asthma attack. Her Ventolin inhaler was empty. Girl's doctor had refused a refill saying that she was using it too frequently." Margo shook her head.

Kane noticed.

"Feel bad remembering that?"

"No. But when something literally makes no sense, I experience what I call a Watson quiver. When it searches for some acceptable meaning and doesn't find it, I can feel a sort of confused shiver. Like it doesn't know what to do. I tell it that such information is not in its databases. Somehow it finds that reassuring."

"Your Watson needs comforting?" Kane asked in disbelief.

"It's just an expression. It takes my response as a signal that no explanation is likely available."

Kane stared at her assistant.

"Your relationship is complicated."

"Yes, it is," Margo agreed. "When we arrived at the house of the dead girl her weeping mother explained that the doctor had nixed a refill. My Watson worked on that for days without finding an explanation for his behavior. Can't tell you how many times *I* shook my head."

"Did you interview the doctor?"

"Yes. He cried. Said he was responsible. Hadn't looked at the girl's chart. Just routinely denied the early refill. Two days later Stone and I were sent to his house again. He had shot himself to death. *That* my Watson comprehended instantly."

"How did Stone react to the child's death?

"Straight-faced and silent."

"Tough guy?"

"Selfish guy. As long as things didn't happen to *him*, he was fine. Thought he was the perfect cop."

"How did he react when he was stabbed by his adulterous partner?"

"He wasn't happy about it."

"You watched him die?"

"It was quick. Heartbeat ceased after he'd bled out."

"Did he say anything?"

"No. He frowned and died silently," Margo replied.

"Perfect cop after all."

"Think so?"

"Yes," Kane confirmed. "If it had been me, I would have been swearing up a storm on *my* way out."

"I like that better," Margo told her. "Then you'd die as a person. Not as a cop."

"What the hell, God?" Kane cried, acting out her imagined exit. "Who the mother fuck decided it was my turn to die? Goddamnit! Goddamnit! Son of a bitch! Quick! Somebody get me a drink!"

"Your last words?"

"My *choice* of last words for sure. I've practiced them for years. Just have to make sure I don't get shot in the fucking throat."

Margo laughed. Kane laughed. And snorted.

"What about you?" she asked Margo.

"No preferences," Margo answered. "I certainly haven't practiced anything."

"Well, let me assure you that if you die hitched to me in this partnership," Kane said, "*I'll* be making up your last words on the report."

Margo gazed at her and thought about that.

"Such as?" she asked, curious.

"What about wilco?" Kane offered.

"Too bland."

"Too bland? You're *programmed* to be bland," Kane teased.

"Well, I don't like wilco."

"What about she died like she lived. No feelings about it one way or the other."

"That's accurate," Margo replied. "But it seems empty."

"Good for you!" Kane told her. "What about, with a haircut and make-up, all she needed next were breasts."

"Now *that* I think is good," Margo remarked.

Kane smiled and winked.

"Well, then let's hope you don't die today. You need to be fitted with your new tits before you exit this vale of tears."

Margo stared at Kane. It just didn't get any more thoughtful than that.

CHAPTER TWENTY-TWO

There were two uniformed policemen and two medics waiting in the Haight apartment where the girls' bodies had been found. Kane walked in, said hello to the cops, and was led to the bedroom where the dead girls were. They were lying face down on a double bed. Naked. Hands and feet tied behind their backs to their necks by white cords.

Kane bent down, turned their heads, and looked at their faces. Asian girls. Chinese. Maybe Korean. Their faces were broad. Their expressions were panic-stricken. Kane rolled both of them over. Maybe *not* teenagers. Nipples without breasts. Silky pubic hair barely there. She tugged at the cords around their necks. They were tight, but there were no marks on their necks to indicate choking or hanging.

Kane stood up and turned to the policeman standing beside her. Black cop. Ernie Jefferson. Had two pre-teen girls of his own. She could see the anger in his eyes.

"Suffocation?" she asked. "I don't see any marks on their necks."

"The marks are inside their throats," Jefferson replied. "Medics did an oral cavity search for obstructions and found that both girls had severe damage—broken bones, lacerations, bleeding—in their mouths and throats. They were likely reamed with a blunt instrument and as they bled to death, then someone inserted their penis in their throat and held their nostrils shut."

"The ropes?" Kane asked.

"Props," Jefferson answered. "You're the detective, not me, but I'd bet my money that this was a snuff shoot."

Margo stepped forward and spoke up.

"Data says that this is not the first instance of such a death in the city."

Jefferson nodded his head.

"There was a woman performing in a professional porn video who was tied up and gagged with the actor's penis down her throat," he said. "She had a brain seizure and died. Not really the same thing."

Kane turned to Margo.

"Did these girls live here?"

"Face recognition software shows that one of them did," Margo answered. "The other was her next-door neighbor. Everyone in this complex needs to be interviewed immediately regarding any disturbances, as well as strangers observed in or around the building. I'll send pictures and texts to you officers, and I would recommend that you call in back-up to begin the interviews as quickly as possible."

Margo paused, then went on.

"Both girls lived with their parents, all of whom are at work. The neighbor girl who came over had a teenage brother." Margo looked at the two cops standing listening to her. "Do you know how these girls were discovered?"

Jefferson answered.

"We were six blocks away when Dora dispatched us after a 911 contact. They'll have a recording of the call."

Yes, they will, Margo thought, and pulled it up out of today's 911 files. She listened to it in her head. The voice of an unidentified boy said that two girls had been killed. He declined to provide his name when asked, but he gave the address where the homicide had occurred and ended the call. The 911 operator had identified the mobile number for the cell phone the caller used. Chuck Yang. Fourteen-year-old brother of the dead girl from next door.

Margo shared the information. One of the officers left to check outside the apartment building while Jefferson called for extra officers to canvas the people in the building and the surrounding neighborhood stores and residences. Margo looked at the dead girls. She felt the skin on one's chest. Still warm. Then she bent her elbow joint. No rigor mortis. She touched her eyelids. Moist and flexible. She checked the other girl. Exactly the same condition. These girls had been dead less than half an hour.

Kane's mobile phone rang. It was the officer who'd gone outside. He had found the naked body of a young Asian male in one of the waste dumpsters. His hands and feet were tied behind him, eyes open and mouth taped shut. He had been stabbed multiple times in the throat, chest, and face and left in the dumpster to die. His clothes were piled in the alley. There were no bloodstains. He had been stripped and murdered. His mobile phone was in his pants pocket. It belonged to Chuck Yang, the boy who had called 911.

Kane called in the murder and told Margo that she was going to attempt to locate the parents of the dead girl and boy. She wanted to intercept them, and, if possible, prevent them from coming home before the bodies were removed. Margo gave Kane their work addresses and watched her partner.

Kane had tears in her eyes. How do you tell a mother and a father that both of their young children had been taken away from them? But she knew that she had to find them and tell them exactly that. She could only imagine the magnitude of their loss and wanted to make sure that they were protected from the sight of their children's molested bodies.

Kane looked at Margo who stood silently waiting for orders.

"Call Dora and tell her that I am going to try and locate the parents of the neighbor girl and her brother. Ask her to assign a team to find the parents of the other girl. The one who lived in this apartment. Please stay here until the police coroner is done and the bodies are removed." Then Kane walked out of the apartment, heading for a task even worse than looking at the tortured corpses of murdered children.

The police coroner arrived dressed in white doctor's scrubs along with two assistants wearing blue pants and blue smocks. Their outfits denoted the hierarchy to which they belonged. The expert examined the bodies. Then the two flunkies wiped up urine and excrement and bagged the corpses. The doctor was an overweight older white male. The assistants were young Hispanic men. Welcome to America.

Margo decided to check the apartment next door where Chuck Yang and his sister had lived.

She asked Officer Jefferson if it had been inspected. He said no. Margo walked down the hall to the adjacent unit. She knocked. No answer. She knocked again. No answer. The door was not locked. Had Chuck Yang gone there after he'd called 911?

Margo turned the knob and entered. The apartment was dark. Curtains and shades were drawn. Margo opened them. Sun entered the room. The living room was filled with shabby, but clean, furniture.

Gold leather sofa. Two terracotta-colored overstuffed chairs. A worn six-by-nine carpet with birds and bees woven into it. There was an old china closet against one wall filled with red carnival glass. Grandmother's treasure? Willed to her granddaughter? Another wall held a large screen television. The screen was dark and its remotes were sitting on a scuffed walnut coffee table with a glass top.

There was a hall past the living room. Margo walked down it. She looked into an empty bedroom. Pink bedspread. Plushies and decorative pillows spread on top. Then a bathroom. Then a room with the door shut. Margo turned the knob to pushed to open it. It was blocked on the other side. She forced it open a few inches. She saw bare feet bathed in blood. She went to find Officer Jefferson. The coroner's work had only just begun.

CHAPTER TWENTY-THREE

Margo called Kane. She hadn't made it to the dead girl's father's place of employment.

"I heard the bulletin on the department channel," Kane told Margo. "The parents never left for work, did they?"

"No. Both of them were stabbed to death in their apartment. Just before or just after their daughter and son were killed."

"What's with all the stabbing?" Kane asked sounding genuinely puzzled.

"It doesn't make any sounds," Margo responded.

"As if anyone in the Haight would report gunshots." Kane paused. "Want me to come back, or can you get a way home?"

"I'll take a cab."

"Any thoughts so far?"

"No. Lots of questions though," Margo replied. "These are two distinct *sets* of murders. The snuff killings of the two Asian girls. And the executions of the neighbor girl's parents and their son. He came home. Saw what had happened to the girls. And called 911. Why didn't he give 911 his name? Was he somehow involved in the girls' murders? Had the murderers been waiting for him and killed his parents in order to neutralize them? Did one group of murderers kill everyone? Or were there separate motives and separate killers?"

"How are you going to proceed?" Kane asked.

"I'll find out all that I can about the deceased. Then I'll identify who lives here, and around here, and see if anyone stands out as a person of interest."

"Probably everyone in the whole damn neighborhood."

"Probably not," Margo corrected Kane. "Then I'll talk to the coroner about his observations. Any male fluids in the females? Any foreign DNA identified? Anything that reminded him of other victims?"

"All right," Kane said. "I'll be at headquarters. Call me when you're done."

Margo sat down in a chair in the apartment and ran IDs on the surrounding neighbors. Every person who paid rent or owned a house anywhere in San Francisco was in the police database. She'd read once that decades ago there had been a lot of citizen concern about privacy vis-à-vis government snooping. It wasn't a concern anymore. Because there was no such thing as privacy. Now even the local 7-11 could access information about where everyone lived, worked, and shopped.

The key to using the endless information was knowing how to filter it. How to sharpen internet queries to pull up the *desired* information. Net neutrality had died about the time Jimmy Carter had, and now internet responses to user queries were filled in with sponsored websites, print and video commercials, and pictures of the underwear you might have considered buying earlier in the week.

The police department had a closed, secure, and commercial-free internet for its officers to use. Margo accessed that with her user ID and password. She called up records on the residents of this part of the Haight. The majority of the males had criminal records. From domestic violence to home robbery and car theft. A lot of women did as well. Sentenced to prison time for drug use, shoplifting, and child neglect. None of the parents of today's dead children had a record. Neither did their kids. After using a wide variety of search criteria, Margo found herself without a suspect in the Haight.

It had been a year since there had been a homicide in the neighborhood. It had occurred when a whore killed her pimp. In a rare triumph of justice, the court declared that the prostitute had acted in self-defense. Further, it awarded her and the other women managed by the pimp appropriate divisions of his estate based on the length of time they had worked for him. There was no police record or journalistic follow up that revealed how the women did afterwards. Hopefully, they went on to better lives than the majority of lottery winners who wound up homeless after a stretch of binge spending.

She reviewed crimes in San Francisco by types of weapons used. Most serious crimes—armed robbery and murder—were associated with guns. Assault rifles and any other military guns had long disappeared from the streets. They were illegal and almost impossible to buy. Handguns were also very rare, ever since California had mandated that *all* pistols had to be purchased from public retail vendors. There were no *legal* private sales of guns. Gun buyers were profiled. Their backgrounds thoroughly checked. And the final purchase information downloaded to police data banks across the nation.

Not surprisingly, a relatively new crime was home invasion *in search of handguns*. The once private list of gun owners had been hacked continuously and was finally just made available for a fee from California to anyone wishing to purchase it. Saved the police records from being constantly hacked which was not hard to do. Most San Francisco government and law enforcement agencies had old, outdated computer devices, layered into ever older stacks of hardware and software. Like coral formations, generation after generation of stuff accreted on top of an existing pile of electronic stuff. The Watson AIs were the only updated computers the police used, and they were thirty years old.

IBM owned the services of the AIs, which in effect meant that they owned the AIs. They rented their Watson-enabled replicants to those who could afford to lease them. As lab-produced parahumans, the courts had yet to make decisions on what legal rights these products had. No AI had ever filed a court case to determine which rights—if any—that robots were entitled to.

They lived with the unofficial, but very real societal belief that AIs were not people, but robots. Replicants. Cyborgs. It wasn't because they didn't have souls. No one believed in souls. It was because they were organic super computers embedded in artificially created bodies. Who was going to argue that *those* things were human? IBM wouldn't. The courts hadn't. And it didn't matter what the AIs thought.

Margo didn't mind. She knew she was programmed not to mind. And she didn't. She also didn't care that she didn't care. What she did care about, however, was not *looking* like a soulless robot anymore. She had dialed up her sensitivity settings about her appearance, directing herself to care about how she looked ever since she had first decided that she looked too bland and too sexless to be female.

Now her hair was cute. Her make-up was feminine. Her breast implants were on the horizon. Interestingly, after she had searched the internet about breast implants, constant pop-ups appeared on her computer screen when she was online offering links to female testimonies about their personal experiences receiving artificial vaginas and adjusting to the hormone therapies required before and after such surgery.

Margo had already done her research. Most of the hormones used were female sexual endocrines taken in conjunction with the surgical structuring of a vulva, a clitoris, and a vagina. The hormones were employed to make the new female labia feel womanly. The vaginal work was done to allow the transgender female to have penetration coitus with a male. Margo wasn't sure that female hormones would work on her. She also wasn't sure that being entered by a man's erect penis was worth the required surgery.

Then again, many naturally existing women seemed to like sex. Statistics said that even women in their eighties wanted to have coitus every week. Lesbian women apparently liked sex equally well, and often practiced penetration using sexual devices. Margo didn't have to wonder if Kane liked sex. The detective looked as if she had been enjoying it as far back as when other girls were learning to read. She had probably passed on her first mobile phone in order to buy a vibrator instead. Margo wasn't judging her. Just trying to get a gauge of how her partner's sexual appetite might work. Her Watson assured her that Kane's appetites were likely very impressive.

After an hour of work on the police internet Margo still had no leads on the slain girls. The coroner sat down on the sofa next to her and reviewed his observations. He was a slight soft-spoken man with perfectly groomed hair and nails. There was nothing he shared that Margo hadn't already suspected. Rape. Knives. Blunt instruments. Death by dying painfully and horribly. He wanted to know if she had any questions before he authorized the medics to remove the bodies.

"I assume that you will perform complete autopsies at head-quarters?" Margo asked.

The coroner nodded.

"And any renegade DNA will be matched against WWW genetic libraries," he told her.

Almost every person in the civilized world had had their DNA samples read and recorded on the day of their birth. If any sperm, or semen, or DNA had rubbed off when the killers had touched, carried, or hurt the victims in these murders, the DNA evidence would be all that she needed to find them. At this point, Margo had nothing else. And if there was no recoverable DNA, then she had nothing at all.

CHAPTER TWENTY-FOUR

Kane called Margo. She wanted to pick her up and go for a drink. She said she felt drained. Margo was still in the Haight and told Kane that any time after she got home would be fine. Kane said she'd be by Margo's at sixish and punched OFF. Margo pulled up a Watson definition for drained. *To withdraw or draw off a liquid gradually.* That didn't seem right. Watson offered a secondary definition. *Whatever a person is dealing with that has drained them to the point where they cannot feel the emotions they'd normally feel when encountering a situation or subject where they would react strongly.*

Margo searched for restoration methodologies. Drinking was not listed. Eating a meal with a friend was, however. Maybe she could invite Kane to dinner after she'd had her drink. Drained didn't sound like a good thing. It often seemed to Margo that humans experienced *everything* through their emotions. *Or* as a television preacher had once famously declared, they experienced everything through their *worst* emotions and desires. He called them The Seven Deadly Sins.

As an AI dedicated to finding murderers, she had to admit that the clergy's point was starkly accurate. She'd been involved in homicides pegged precisely to the worst embodiments of every one of those sins. Deadly was not a misnomer.

Pride. Defending to the death an inflated opinion of one's self. Greed. Committing murder in order to steal money or goods from someone else. Lust. Desire fulfilled by forcing an unwilling partner to yield even to the point of dying. Wrath. Uncontrolled anger leading to all kinds of violent behaviors. Envy. Inability to forgive another for their good fortune and killing them for it. Gluttony. Wanting food or drink so much that violence is resorted to in order to seize it. Sloth. Failure to act or help a victim in need, resulting in their death. This last one was by far the most prevalent sin of the lot. Yet its dreadful consequences were often ignored because it was the most *passive* deadly sin of the lot.

Margo walked outside to the front of the apartment building and watched the ambulances depart.

Then the coroner's wagon. Then the two black and whites. With the black and whites inside. Was that racist? She wasn't racist. But her Watson insisted that at the very least that thought could be interpreted as disrespectful.

The police had taped off the bedrooms with yellow crime scene tape. The dumpster where Yang's body had been discovered was taped as well. Forensics had been there and would be back. Initial evidence often led to more questions and repeat visits. The coroner had taken another moment on his way out to tell Margo that he didn't think there were any male fluids in the girls' vaginas or anuses. But he had swabbed their mouths and throats because of the kind of abuse they'd endured and had found a lot of residues.

Margo called for a taxi. They were self-driven automobiles and were widely available. She thought about the two dead girls.

Harboring sperm or semen in their mouths and throats. Maybe there were angels waiting in heaven to help them clean up the moment they arrived. They certainly wouldn't be the first females to enter paradise needing male seed removed from one orifice or another.

As she rode home Margo reflected on the random and violent deaths she had encountered as a homicide assistant. No matter the age of the individual, life was fragile, and police witnessed it terminated abruptly again and again. Her former partner, Drake Stone—now involuntarily retired by Barbara Fasten's knitting needle—had once mused out loud that he was always amazed when he witnessed a life extinguished in a moment.

"It's all just like Jimmy Hoffa's death in the old Scorsese movie *The Irishman,*" Stone had told her. "Hoffa was larger than life. Famous and powerful. With tens of thousands of loyal union truck drivers under his thumb. Then he lost it. Two .38 slugs to the back of his head. Bang! Bang! That's all that it took."

Stone had left Margo at the coffee shop where they had stopped and had gone off somewhere on his own to get drunk. He didn't report to work the next day. Perhaps he was sleeping off the horror of his revelation from the day before. Someone in the cosmos snaps their fingers and you die. One could try and explain it as God, or karma, or just bad luck, but the fact was you died. Ready or not.

Kane had largely regained her normal spirits by the time she arrived. Margo got in the Acura and looked at her partner.

"You appear to be doing better," she commented.

"Yeah," Kane agreed and started backing her car up. "Took an extra hundred grams of Zoloft and I feel better. Not sure if that extra shit has taken effect yet, but even if this is just a placebo high I'll take it." Kane laughed, almost sounding hysterical.

Margo took a teraflop to check on Zoloft overdoses. She found forty-two reported U.S. cases caused by overdosing fifty to eight thousand milligrams more than prescribed. Elevated blood pressure. Hallucinations. Seizures. Coma. She looked at Kane. There was no evidence of any of those adverse reactions. But she *was* acting like she was high. Like she had OD'd on coffee. Or cocaine. Kane began humming. She grinned and looked at Margo. Her pupils were as dark and large as a lunar eclipse. Cocaine.

"It all just got to me," Kane said and shook her head. "Dead parents. Dead boy. Dead girls. Dead as a result of the worst circumstances." Kane glanced at Margo. Her AI was looking out the front windshield. "Did you examine the boy's body?" she asked. Margo nodded. "Was there any discernable pattern to the stab wounds?" Margo nodded her head. "Describe them," Kane ordered.

"There were fifty-seven wounds," Margo began. "The boy had been stripped and tied up. He was probably held by one person while another stabbed his torso over and over."

"Held how?"

"By the arms. From behind. There were wounds in his chest, abdomen, sides, shoulders, neck, and face. There were no wounds in his arms. The stabbing sequence can be reconstructed to show that the initial wounds were inflicted in such a way as to avoid major blood veins, arteries, and internal organs. The length of the blade was five inches and only the last six blows were life-threatening. They were deliberately executed against the lungs, the blood veins in the neck, and the heart itself."

"How long did it take him to die?"

"He was alive until those last fatal wounds. He bled a lot. His body was covered in blood. Dripping out of his injuries and soaking his chest, legs, and the pavement. However, it was the final blow that truly ended his life and was probably instantly mortal."

"A *coup de grâce*?" Kane asked.

"Very possibly. His heart was stabbed in the center and then the knife was pulled down along a rib. Cut the heart into two pieces."

"In your estimate, what was the point of the torture?"

"The boy's mouth was taped. But his eyes were left uncovered. In similar killings a large mirror was used to force the victim to watch his own torture and death."

"What kind of similar killings?"

"Organized crime executions. Drug users who failed to pay for their dope. It is a punishment methodology favored by crime families in eastern European countries and Russia."

Kane thought about possibilities.

"The kid may have been killed over drugs?" she asked.

"Yes. The autopsy will show whatever he had in his body."

"And his murder was separate from the snuff killings?"

"I think it was," Margo replied. "The parents had their throats cut. I think that *their* killings were unplanned. Perhaps they were home when the killers came looking for their son. The murders of the two girls appear to be a separate occurrence. They were killed for a pornographic snuff video."

"Then we're talking two sets of killers working at the same time in the same building?" Kane asked. She'd never heard of that kind of coincidence.

"Yes," Margo answered. "One set making a snuff video. The other set punishing a debtor."

"For fuck's sake," Kane murmured. "What a day."

Margo looked at her.

"What a species," she said.

CHAPTER TWENTY-FIVE

Kane wanted to eat at a Mel's Drive In.

"I've never been to one of those," Margo told her.

"You'll love it," Kane told her. "All-American burgers and fries. And the best orange sherbet in the universe."

Margo checked her Watson.

"They only offer beer and wine," she told Kane. "Are you okay with that?"

"Fuck no," Kane spat out. "Only morons drink beer. And only sissies drink wine. What else do they have?"

"You mean non-alcoholic beverages?" Margo asked. She knew that Kane usually preferred to drink chardonnay.

"Just tell me what they've got," Kane replied sounding pissed.

"Coke, Diet Coke, root beer, Sprite, Evian, San Pellegrino, iced tea, tea, hot chocolate with whipped cream, lemonade, cappuccino, soy, almond, or regular milk, espresso, café latte, café mocha, iced cappuccino, espresso milk shake, coffee, brewed decaf, iced coffee—"

"Stop," Kane ordered. "There's a liquor store up ahead on Geary. I'll get some whiskey and we'll have Irish coffees. You know there used to be a place on the old waterfront called Buena Vista Café. Claimed to be the first place in America to serve Irish coffees." Kane shrugged. "Don't know if that was true, but I sure liked to stop in there."

Margo didn't say anything. She had never had an Irish coffee. And she had never heard of the Buena Vista Café. She checked it. A corner café across the street from where the now defunct cable cars had a manual turnaround. Cable car drivers got out and pushed the cars one hundred and eighty degrees around to face the return direction. Watson told her that a high percentage of cable car drivers drank at Buena Vista after a turn-around. Did that matter? Didn't look like they had much of a challenge to hook onto or off of the moving underground cable that pulled the cars. Could they do it under the influence? Apparently, they could.

Kane stopped at a small liquor store and bought a pint of Jameson Irish Whiskey. Then she drove to Mel's and pulled into a no parking zone. She led Margo into the restaurant. It looked like the retro hamburger joints featured in 1950s and 1960s movies. Padded booths. Long counter with stools. A fast-talking young man with thick hair on top and shaved sides showed them to the counter. He was wearing white pants, a white shirt, white shoes, and a folded white paper hat. He seated them and placed large plastic menus in front of them. He said someone would take their order right away.

"A coffee *now*," Kane told him before he could escape. He grinned and immediately returned with a mug of coffee, a bowl of sugar and sweetener packs, and a small metal pitcher of cream. Kane took out her pint of whiskey. She added a slug to her coffee. Then she drank a big gulp. "I know what I want to order," she told Margo. "It was called a patty melt when I was a kid. Slab of cooked hamburger on toasted rye, a shitload of American cheese, and a heap of grilled onions."

Margo rarely ate beef and preferred chicken. Mel's Creole fried chicken sandwich on brioche served with cold slaw caught her eye. She liked anything Creole. Spicy and sometimes blackened, the cooking traced its roots back to a community of mulattoes residing—but never fully accepted—in New Orleans. She could relate. She felt like a Creole in the San Francisco Police Department. Useful, but never really liked. Did Kane like her? Too early to tell. Stone had hated her. He told her that she was plain to look at, and boring to listen to. He didn't admit it, but he put up with Margo because of her knack of finding the bad guys. For which he took credit.

Kane drank three Irish coffees and avoided talking about the five bodies the city had yielded up this morning. Margo wouldn't bring up any work issues if Kane was not in the mood. Her partner's emotional blockade was obvious. She wanted protection from feeling *anything* tonight. Margo wondered if Kane's rational mind continued to work on its own agenda even when her emotional intelligence was overwrought.

Margo's mind was continually active and unimpeded by emotion upset. Her interest in understanding human emotions diminished significantly every time she witnessed Kane's loss of self-control. Or Sergeant Concepcion's tantrums. Or the foul deeds committed by emotionally wayward criminals.

Kane ate and drank in silence. Margo finished her Creole chicken sandwich and reviewed the coroner's autopsy findings filed with her Watson, trying to establish a chronology of when and how the multiple murders had been committed in the Haight. She settled on a chronology but would wait to tell her partner tomorrow. She suspected that neither the criminal quick nor the refrigerated dead had significant plans prior to her morning coffee with Kane.

Kane was late. Margo viewed the morning television news reports of yesterday's homicides. Videos showed multiple bodies covered by blankets. The city was shaken by the murders, particularly of the three children. There were panicky demands from the city's school board, police watchdog groups, and residents of the Haight that the killers be caught and punished. It would happen. Margo was sure of that. But the end was not in sight.

Kane sat and watched the television reporting after she arrived. Margo served her coffee and wheat toast, which her partner ate with butter and grape jelly. After seeing segments about the murders play on several channels, Kane looked at Margo.

"You've established a timeline for the murders by now I would guess. *Si?*"

"Yes. I have a plausible work up," Margo responded.

"Please."

"The coroner released autopsy reports last night," Margo began. "Chuck Yang's cadaver held significant amounts of fentanyl, diazepam, and heroin. His body surfaces yielded several DNA samples where one killer held his arms and where the other rubbed his hand against his skin while stabbing him. The two men involved in that murder have been identified by DNA records on file, and warrants have been issued for their arrest. Both are young second-generation Serbian Americans. No criminal sheets, but likely affiliated with the Serbian mob here or overseas.

"I believe those same two men murdered Yang's father and mother," Margo went on. "The parents were home when the narcotics dealers arrived looking for their son. Next door in the neighboring apartment the *other* killers were making their snuff video. They somehow intercepted the drug enforcers and struck a deal to video them murdering the Yang boy. I don't know where he was when he called in the 911 report on his sister, but shortly after he made that call, he was apprehended by the drug dealers and stabbed him to death with the camera rolling."

Margo saw that Kane was taking it all in. She paused for a moment and then went on.

"There were traces of sperm and seminal fluids in the mouths and throats of both dead girls. The genetic samples indicate that the men are likely from eastern Europe or Central Asia. Turkic and Mongol ancestry. But at this point there is no way to specifically identify them. There were no profiles that matched their DNA in any police files across the globe."

"So, you were right," Kane responded. "Two sets of killers. Two different agendas. Then coming together at Chuck Yang's execution." Kane rested her elbow on the table and put her chin in her hand. "What next?" she asked.

"Both snuff videos will be edited and made available to internet viewers," Margo answered. "For a price. A big price I would guess. The public internet serves about eight percent of worldwide web users. The deep internet handles most traffic. It serves about ninety percent of internet users with unregistered sites and encrypted language that public search engines cannot access.

"Last, there is the so-called dark internet. It serves about two percent of users. Those with specific tastes for the immoral, the illegal, and the unthinkable. Like the videos of our victims' murders. The dark internet can only be accessed by private search engines that encrypt users' IDs and the sites they visit. That encourages users to think that they are anonymous and that their searches are protected. Not likely. It has to be tempting for some providers to sell the user's IDs and passwords to hackers who know that customers routinely use the same info to access their own computers and applications.

"Our next step," Margo continued, "is to use the clean police computers—registered under false names yet linked to valid payment options—to search the dark web for the appearance of the two snuff videos. Once they are online, we will investigate the sites where they appear, their locations, and the payment entities they use, working through the layers of details until we discover the perps and their business locations."

"You can do that?" Kane said amazed.

"No," Margo answered. "But Watson can."

Kane stared at her homicide assistant.

"My God," she muttered. "What a burden you must carry knowing your capabilities."

Margo didn't answer. She did think that she was powerful. If she had functioning emotions she might feel that she was unstoppable.

CHAPTER TWENTY-SIX

S o, you want to watch some dirty movies?" Sergeant
Concepcion asked. Kane had gone to her superior to get
access to the department's clean computers. Its dark internet computers. She had not asked Margo to go with her figuring
that Concepcion would be on better behavior if her AI assistant
was not present.

"Only if it doesn't interfere with *your* scheduled time," Kane
responded.

Concepcion frowned.

"What is that smart ass comment supposed to mean?" he
growled.

Kane ignored him.

"I need to find two snuff videos that were made at the
Haight killings. The only way I can do that is to search the dark
web. Unless you've seen them already."

"You're getting my dander up, Kane," Concepcion reacted
angrily.

"Sorry, sir," Kane said. "But I have three homicides that are
directly linked to those snuff videos and I need access to the
dark internet."

"Well, you won't get it by pissing me off." Concepcion crossed his arms and sat back in his desk chair.

"I didn't mean to, sir," Kane lied.

Concepcion had on a navy business suit, a white shirt, and a blue-and-gray paisley tie. Kane was wearing a taupe suit, a white blouse, and four-inch brown heels. The sergeant thought that a snuff video starring Detective C. Kane would be worth searching for. Although he'd prefer to see Margo Humanot in such a role. Hell, even just a plain old murder would be fine in her case.

"How are you doing with your AI?" he asked.

"What do you think, sir?" Kane replied. She paused a moment and went on. "You know that her work yesterday resulted in the identification and arrests today of the two men who were responsible for the murder of the dead boy and his parents."

Concepcion listened. He declined to comment.

"She's good, Sergeant," Kane went on. "Smarter and faster than any cop she's ever worked for. Including me."

"I'm not sure how big a compliment that is," Concepcion remarked.

Kane reacted strongly.

"How the fuck did you ever get this promotion?" she said loudly. "You're good at being an asshole. What were the other requirements for the job?"

"Ha!" Concepcion burst out and laughed. "I got it because I keep you and your compadres in line. I love to bust your chops, Kane. Makes you and every other homicide detective in this insane asylum humble. Humble gets results. Thinking that your shit don't stink doesn't catch the perps." The sergeant grinned and waited for Kane's retort. It didn't come. He narrowed his eyes and searched her face. "What?" he finally snapped.

"That actually sounds somewhat logical," Kane conceded. "God knows you're good at it."

"*And* damnit," Concepcion added, "you can check out the homicide department's arrests and convictions if you don't think it works."

"Okay," Kane capitulated. "So, what about the dark internet access?"

"Go talk to the chief. Tell him it's urgent and that I will schedule unlimited time for exploring the dark web for the next seven days." Concepcion leaned forward over his desk and folded his hands. "Nothing happens in a week you get to come and see me again."

"Thank you, Sergeant," Kane said. She smiled thinking how remarkable it was that Concepcion could stay in character day after day as homicide's worst jerk.

He smiled back.

Police Chief Oakes authorized twelve-hour segments on one of the force's unregistered computers for seven consecutive days. If, in fact, dark web search engines truly encrypted users' information, then using a so-called clean computer didn't matter. However, if the providers lied and sold users' identifications and passwords to cash-flush hackers, the clean police computer would identify itself as being owned by a false entity with all personal and payment details fabricated as well. And yet the information would appear valid and the computer address would pay as required. The San Francisco Police Department didn't do everything perfectly, but they had done a pretty respectable job preparing officers to investigate criminal materials logged onto dark internet channels.

Kane and Margo sat at the computer. Margo was at the keyboard.

"Okay, partner," Kane said. "What are the rules?"

"To start, we follow the initial user protocols," Margo answered. "We set up an account with a user ID and a password. Then fund an XRP account in ripple cryptocurrency, which the webmasters charge for browsing access. Ten to thirty ripples a month. Right now, the value of a ripple is close to that of a dollar."

"Mega cheap to get to drill for nasty stuff," Kane commented.

"Yes. To *browse* for nasty stuff. But viewing the nasty stuff is the expensive part. Videos start at two hundred ripples in XRP currency and goes up from there depending on what you watch. Sites offering self-mutilation may charge five hundred. Involuntary mutilation starts at a thousand. Twenty-five hundred to watch a rape. Five thousand or more to watch a murder like Chuck Yang's. Short and bloody. Watson has found snuff episodes with deep throating until suffocation at 10,000 per. Again, paid in XRP ripples."

"Is this a rich man's game?" Kane asked.

"Yes," Margo answered. "And *that* bothers me. Those viewers have money. Which likely means they have power. Might be the CEO you know. Or the lawyer you use."

"Or maybe even some software geek with a bunch of Google stock options," Kane offered.

"Don't knock those guys," Margo said. "We may wind up contracting some of those boy geniuses to drill into the encrypted protection of the sites to nail the owners."

Kane nodded. If she actually ever did meet a young engineer with big Google options, she'd probably ask him if he wanted to trade some of those shares for the chance to do it with a dyke. She grinned. Margo looked at her. She stopped grinning.

Margo queried for search engines for the dark web. Three came up. She picked the one her Watson believed to be the most reliable in terms of providing real sites and real experiences. A standard-looking form appeared on the monitor asking for information to be filled in. Margo used the ID and password the police Information Technology manager had provided. The browser asked for crypto currency account information as well as stating that the account would be charged ten XRP crypto ripples every day regardless of access frequency. Or if there was no access at all. It didn't ask for contact details.

There was a paragraph stating that the internet provider took no responsibility for site content and any depictions of an offbeat nature. *Offbeat?* thought Kane. Offbeat was the stuff people did in their bedroom. The activities she expected to encounter here were more in the category of what put people in hell. If there was a God, he was surely blowing through every encrypted ID and taking down names.

Margo entered yes to a query asking if she had read the provider's disclaimer, then entered the financial information requested.

A pop-up window immediately welcomed her back as an active user.

"I should have thought of that," Margo said. "I tried to create a new account when there was already an active one on this site."

"Does that make any difference?" Kane asked.

"Not on regular internet sites. They dump the redundant application and use the one that's already active. On this internet, however, the provider may be concerned that an unauthorized user is trying to enter using someone else's ID. Probably won't question it this first time. But will likely respond with a warning and/or blocked access if it happens again."

Margo looked at Kane.

"What trial activity would you like to view?"

"What do you mean?" Kane asked confused.

"We're going to surf a lot of dark waves before we get around to asking about snuff videos. So, we'll start with simple searches. Legal activities. Still not necessarily for the squeamish. It may be of a fetish nature. Something to do with bondage. Or needles, clips, ice, even cuts." Margo saw that Kane was still not sure what to ask for. Evidently, she was not too kinky. Margo smiled. A straight lesbian.

"How about a tattoo job?" Kane finally asked.

"Sure."

"On a shaved pussy."

Margo looked over at Kane's face.

"Thinking about getting one?" she asked.

"Maybe," Kane answered. Then she smiled and winked.

Do Androids Dream of Electric Sheep?

Margo had dreams that night that it was she who had the tattoo placed on her cunny. She didn't know what the artwork looked like. Turned out it didn't matter. Just thinking about the tattoo propelled Margo into her own thoughts about having female sexual parts. She dreamed about using a vibrator. She dreamed about a lover giving her cunnilingus. A man. Then a woman. Then she dreamed about becoming pregnant. More than anything else that was what she really wanted to experience. Sexual intimacy was pleasure. Sexual impregnation was power. The power to create another human being.

She dreamed that she asked her Watson to provide files on pregnancy and birth. She wondered if her Watson was beginning to sense that such interests were starkly alien to her basic existence as a replicant. When she asked for those specific materials, her Watson asked, Why?

CHAPTER TWENTY-SEVEN

The tattooing video was eye-opening. Margo decided that she never wanted a tattoo *anywhere* on her body. Kane was still open to tats—as she called them—but maybe not on her pubic mound. Whole lot of scratching going on to etch the ink into all three layers of skin. The final result of the tattooing was a heart with a crown of thorns. Ironic and interesting for maybe a glance or two. Jesus with a crown of thorns might have been a more captivating choice for that particular physiognomy.

As the week's viewings progressed, Detective Kane observed a clear escalation of pain in the videos her homicide assistant selected for them to watch. Self-mutilations—arms, chests, tummies, and breasts—cut by knives, scissors, and box cutters. Involuntary cuttings. One teenage girl had her face cut in furrows. One long cut per day over the course of two weeks of recording. Twice during this viewing cycle Kane left to throw up. She was upset at the mutilation, but it was the gagged girl's moans and weeping that made her ill to the point of relieving herself of whatever her breakfast had been.

Where had that girl come from, Kane wondered? Where did she wind up afterwards? She had her answer two days later when Margo found the same young woman featured in a snuff video. It cost 5,500 ripples and neither Kane nor Margo watched all of it. The girl with her face full of cuts—half-healed and still bleeding—was naked, bound to a table, with her hands and feet spread and tied to its four legs.

Then beginning with her neck, new cuts were made with a box cutter. A masked man was administering the wounds, and again the gagged woman groaned and cried with every cut. Hands, feet, arms, legs. Kane turned away when the woman's nipples were sliced off. Margo left the site when the victim's abdomen was opened and her living organs removed.

Kane had to go throw up even though she'd had no breakfast. Afterwards she didn't talk to Margo. She just went home. Margo stayed searching for snuff offerings of the deaths of Chuck Yang or of his sister and her friend. Nothing was posted and there were no photos suggesting availability. Margo did find videos, however, that appeared to be the work of like-minded killers. There were six sessions posted that portrayed men using bound women for sex. Margo watched them all. The women were mature, appearing to be in their twenties or thirties. Two were Asians. One was black. Three were white.

Various sex acts were portrayed, usually beginning with deep throat fellatio, then progressing to vaginal and anal intercourse. The women were naked and tied to beds, tables, sofas, and chairs, but not gagged. They appeared to be barely conscious. They had probably been forced to swallow large doses of roofies—date rape drugs—flunitrazepam, gamma hydroxybutyric acid, or ketamine.

At some point each of the women were videoed lying on their backs while a large male penis was forced into their mouths. A visible bulge was seen as it filled their throats. The penis was held inside until the women began to shake and quiver, struggling to breathe. The penis was withdrawn and reinserted multiple times.

In some videos, objects were jammed down the women's throats. A cooking baster. A large fist. The handle of a baseball bat which caused instant bleeding. The perpetrator reinserted his penis and held it in until the woman choking on it and her own blood died of strangulation. The video closed with a close-up of the victim's face. Her eyes were huge. Her jaw was open and slack. Blood continued to flow from the sides of the dead woman's mouth.

Margo shut off the computer and sat silently thinking about what she had seen. She sat for a very long time. Animals didn't do such things. But humans did. Was it really for the money? Or was it to satisfy acquired appetites? Unnatural appetites. Watson's response to the videos was to suggest that people who were guilty of such depravities were in it for the power. Stripping the victims. Tying them up. Choking them with their sex organs. Taking their sex, their life, and their futures away in a last act of degradation and unbearable pain.

Margo did not have an opinion. But she decided that when she and Kane tracked down the men who had done such things to the Haight girls, they would not live beyond the moment she identified them. It was not an emotional decision. It was justice. Punishment. Annihilation. It wouldn't change anything. But it *would* prevent them from torturing and murdering any more females. She would shoot the man or men responsible and watch them die. Animals didn't do such things. But humans did.

Margo and Kane checked the dark internet for postings of the slain girls' murder three times every day during their seven-day access. There was no video. It had been almost ten days since the double murders had occurred, but there was no video.

"I think the persons who did the video tape found out that the men who tracked down and murdered Chuck Yang have been identified and arrested," Kane suggested. "Afraid that they can be identified by those drug enforcers might just be enough to make them hesitate to post the video of the girls they murdered."

She and Margo were sitting in Kane's office. A closed-door office that detectives used to conduct their business in private. Margo had no office. Or cube. Or desk in the so-called bullpen where a ton of policemen sat when they weren't on the street.

"Well, goddamnit," Kane suddenly hissed. "Goddamnit to hell." Margo sat and waited for an explanation.

Kane looked at her.

"We've can to talk to the men who murdered Chuck Yang," she said. "They saw and maybe even knew the men who killed the girls." Kane stared at Margo for a moment, then spoke. "Where are they being held?"

"They have been transferred from city jail to San Francisco County," Margo told her. "They're awaiting arraignment."

Kane frowned.

"They were apprehended more than a week ago. Why has their arraignment been delayed?"

Watson provided the answer.

"There is virtually no data on them other than the DNA matches. They are Serbian Americans but they don't live in San Francisco. Their history and activities in this country are being researched."

"Freelancers," Kane said with disgust. "In *my* hometown."

"In *jail* in your hometown," Margo reminded her.

"In jail and about to be visited in my hometown," Kane added. She thought about that for a moment. "I'm bringing a pistol," she told Margo. "And one for you. I also want to grab some liquid ecstasy. I can get both from evidence storage."

"Liquid ecstasy?"

"A shot of that and our suspects will mellow out and maybe even feel inclined to help a couple of nice girls like us."

"You're shitting me," Margo commented.

"Just watch," Kane said and smiled.

"And how exactly will you obtain the pistol *and* the illegal drug from evidence?" Margo asked.

"Auggie Blanchard has this shift. He gives me whatever I want for a blowjob."

"You do it right there?"

Kane grinned.

"It's quiet. In the basement. Lockers everywhere. And some dark niches where a boy can be alone with his date."

"*That's* hardly the case."

"Could be if I was straight. He has a big cock. Clean and pretty. And he makes really righteous sounds when he cums."

"That's plenty."

"All righty then." Kane grinned again. "Don't forget who told you this if you ever need anything from the evidence lockers."

Margo used a teraflop imagining blowing Blanchard and witnessing his righteous climax. There were worse ways to invest a teraflop.

CHAPTER TWENTY-EIGHT

Kane made an appointment the next morning with Auggie Blanchard in evidence storage. Concepcion had refused to give her any more time on a clean police computer, so she made sure that she got everything she needed to pursue the murderers off the web.

She brought her items over to Margo's apartment after work and spread them out on her sofa. Margo served her a glass of Talbot chardonnay which she knew that Kane liked, but her partner had already gotten a head start at a bar on the way over and was feeling pretty good about things.

"And here we are," Kane said enthusiastically. She picked up a .32 Smith & Wesson
semi-automatic pistol and held it out to Margo. Margo took it.

"Light, eh?" Kane asked. "Dumb palookas at the department call it a ladies' gun. Fine. Does almost as much damage as a .357 Magnum and doesn't numb your fucking fingers when you pull the trigger. How's it feel?"

"Feels okay."

"Okay enough to shoot someone?"

"If it's a someone who killed the girls, I won't have any problem."

"Those assholes might have colleagues who also need to be taught how to be polite," Kane warned Margo. "Good rule of thumb is that when I tell you to shoot someone, you do it. Period."

Margo handed the pistol back to Kane.

"My Watson won't like that."

"Fuck your Watson. Fix it so you and I decide who gets a bullet from you."

"I can do that."

"Make *sure* that you do that," Kane said somewhat gruffly. "When I tell you to shoot, the person whose life is in the balance may be *mine*. I have to count on you."

Margo nodded.

"I will not fail you."

"Good."

"When you say shoot, *I* am the one who will determine how many times. Is that correct?"

"Yes," Kane agreed. "But err on the side of more is better."

"I understand."

"Dead men don't talk about why they scored extra bullets when being taken down. It's one of the few breaks that cops get. If it's obvious that the perp needed to be dead, no one generally counts how many bullets it took to do the job."

Kane slid the .32 into a fabric shoulder holster and handed it to Margo.

"Wear it under a suitcoat. Practice taking the gun out without shooting yourself. Then practice *whipping* it out, aiming, and pulling the trigger as fast as you can. Here's a box of cartridges. Break the revolver open and load the cylinder. Seven bullets. Practice loading it over and over. You may not need to reload ever, but why not know how to do it? Can I have some more wine?"

Kane drank her wine and explained the other items she had brought. She held up a medical injection gun and showed Margo the cartridges that she would load into it. She said they were filled with liquid ecstasy. Margo knew it by its psychoactive active ingredient, MDMA. Methylenedioxymethamphetamine. It was related to both amphetaminenane and phenletylamine classes of compounds.

Taken in small doses ecstasy increased empathy, emotional openness, and provided a sense of wellbeing. The effects of MDMA were caused by the release of serotonin in the brain. Given in the mega doses Kane intended to administer to the prisoners, it would render them into wonderfully cheerful folks who would babble happily about whatever information they were asked for. Truth serum for happily emptying your heart out.

All ecstasy products had been declared illegal by the US government. The logic was that the drug was a feel-good drug with no medicinal value with a great likelihood of being abused. Law courts had already declared the drug legal, but were countermanded by the Drug Enforcement Agency, which made the drug illegal anyway. Even Margo's Watson—programmed to have a classic "square" personality—declared those actions unnecessary.

American citizens had been perennially offered truly life-threatening substances like alcohol and tobacco, readily available around the clock at every bar, liquor store, and supermarket. But the government saw fit to spare folks from the *positive* effects of MDMA. Margo smiled to herself thinking that she wouldn't mind a shot of the ecstasy herself. Of course, her relaxed demeanor might encourage Kane to make a pass at her. And she'd probably say yes.

Kane left and Margo watched an installment of the latest BBC series on *Planet Earth*. She witnessed the destruction of the final bits of rain forest, was shown the parts of the planet where climate change had created new deserts, and observed the world's empty oceans where no species remained that could be harvested for food in any quantity.

She turned the television off feeling disoriented trying to comprehend what humankind had done to the world. It made her regret that she had not asked Kane for a blast from her ecstasy gun. Well, not really. But she did have to admit that she had a small craving. Probably not very AI-like. But all things considered, she was not all that AI-like in a lot of ways anymore.

Disagreeing and disrespecting Sergeant Concepcion. Being pleased—and vain—looking at her reflection in the make-up mirror. Adjusting her protocols to allow raising her voice, using sarcasm, and laughing if she wanted. Reprogramming herself to shoot guns. And to kill on Kane's command. It had yet to be revealed if these changes were good or bad. And she wasn't done evolving by a long shot. She went to sleep thinking about empty oceans, breast implants, and—as Kane had reminded her when she left—schmoozing with the bad guys at the county jail the next day.

CHAPTER TWENTY-NINE

Kane got permission for Margo and her to visit the two suspects held for killing Chuck Yang and his parents. Kane and Margo checked in at the visitor's desk at county. IDs. Face recognition shots. Retina scans. The new facility—several stories high and constructed without any windows—had been built higher than the elevated Bay, but not so high as to prevent it from being flooded during the most severe storms.

The ACLU took the city to court saying that the rights of prisoners were being violated by being incarcerated in an unsafe building. Cruel and unusual punishment. The courts threw it out, all the way up to the Supreme Court which declined to hear it. No one gave a shit if the prisoners could drown. Or *did* drown. America post-Donald Trump had stopped listening to liberals. The only equal opportunity ever spoken about now in the San Francisco police station was the chance that every prisoner in county would share the same risk of dying come hell or high water. Margo was not political. Kane liked the new America. She wanted hardworking decent citizens to be protected by the police. But not robbers. Not murderers. Not snuffers.

Kane and Margo were escorted to a small windowless room. There was a metal table and four metal chairs. Two policemen went to fetch the prisoners. Margo scanned the room. No security cameras. That was a courtesy pass to conduct their interview any way that she and Kane wanted unless the cops stayed in the room.

The policemen returned with prisoners whose hands were cuffed behind their backs. The murder suspects were well-built young men with big beards and shaved heads. They looked like college kids off the dance club floors. They were wearing orange jumpsuits with their prison numbers sewn on their chests. They both had sullen faces. To cover their fear? Or the result of having knifed so many folks they no longer gave a shit about looking civil?

The two cops walked out after the prisoners sat. They left the door wide open. Kane sat and pulled a small tape recorder out of her purse. Margo sat and looked at the prisoners. They looked back. They knew that Margo was an AI. They had absolutely no interest in looking at her after a first glance. Kane, on the other hand, was worth staring at. She turned the tape recorder on and began speaking.

"So, boys, how are things in here?"

Both men grunted. One of them spit on the floor.

"Doesn't surprise me," Kane said. "Beats taking a dirt nap though, doesn't it? Like the ones you provided for Charles Yang and his parents, Phil and LiLi Yang."

The two men scowled. Bitch.

"I don't actually give a shit about the Yangs," Kane went on. "*Or* you two assholes who killed them. Who I care about are the two perps who videotaped you stabbing the boy to death."

One of the men looked surprised. The other narrowed his eyes and watched.

"Yeah, we figured out what went on. You killed the kid in the alley while the fellas who'd deep throated his sister videoed it. How much did they pay you? Enough to buy beer and cigarettes for a week or two?"

"You have a smart mouth, lady," the wary con said.

Kane smiled.

"It's okay muscle man," she said. "Because I'm no lady."

"Perfect," he sneered in response. "Because your partner ain't no lady, either."

Margo matched his seemingly accent-free speech to language nuances present from a childhood spent with Serbian parents. Watson had identified both men as second-generation Americans. Their fathers and mothers would have thick accents. The prisoner's English mimicked bits and pieces of how they spoke. Maybe he had learned Serbian before English?

"*Isn't*," Kane amended. "Not ain't, prick. And you're wrong. My assistant is a great lady. Tracked you two rejects down after Charles Yang's murder based solely on your DNA. Ever thought about being more careful, retards? And now you're in the slammer until the snuff king whose minions videoed your execution finds out that you're here. Then you'll be hung in your cells right here in county jail. Suicides." Both men began to look uncomfortable. "Because you saw the shits who snuffed the girls."

Kane stroked her chin with her index finger.

"To me you're just two bums waiting to go to trial for murder. But to the man who had the girls kidnapped and murdered, you're *witnesses*. Witnesses to his employees. Murderers who snuffed children. And I suspect that you might even know who that person is. Because wherever *you* come from, *he* comes from."

Both men were clearly feeling some anxiety. Was Kane close to the truth?

Margo stepped in.

"You're American Serbs," she said. "And we aren't the only ones who know."

Now the men began to look fearful despite their tough-guy demeanors. Margo realized that the murderers of the dead girls were probably American Serbs also, or at least Serbs still in the old country, the nation Watson now pinpointed as the location accountable for almost all European dark web snuff videos. The ones made of the murders of Chuck Yang and the girls in the Haight had probably been uploaded from there. She knew where to find them now. Polluting the web from eastern Europe.

"You gentlemen want to talk about anything?" Kane asked. "Off the record?"

"What does off the record mean?" one prisoner asked.

"It means that whatever you tell me won't be recorded, and anything I use to find the girls' killers will not be tracked back to you. Plus, I can offer an extra incentive. I have some hits of MDMA. Ecstasy."

The prisoners looked at each other. Then back at Kane. Both of them nodded. Kane turned off her tape recorder and put it back in her purse. She took out the injector gun and several cartridges. She shot up both men. Within five minutes they were teary-eyed and quite chatty.

"I love you, Igor," one man told the other.

"And I love you, Max," his partner replied. "There is no one I love more." Igor stood up and bent over to give Max a big hug. As his hands were cuffed, he settled for snuggling his face in Max's neck. He sat back down.

"This is a time to love everybody," Kane told them. "But other times it's hard to love, isn't that true?" The men nodded. "I think you know the two men who paid you to let them video the killing of the Chinese boy. They're not very nice people, are they?"

Max shook his head.

"Very lonely men," he said. "Both of them. Frank and Victor," he said.

"I don't think I've met them," Kane said. "Do you know their last names?"

"Frank Boskovic and Victor Nicolic," Max replied. He was turning out to be the talker. "Two sad, lonely men."

"How do you know them?"

"We know their organization and their boss. Harry Milosesvic. Another sad and lonely man."

"But very rich," Igor added. "He's the man behind the world's largest collection of snuff videos. All catalogued in Serbia."

"You don't work for him though?" Kane asked.

Igor shook his head.

"Sad and lonely man."

"But very wealthy," Max added again.

"Why would he have any videos made here?"

"He has men who work for him all over Asia and the US. He does not make his movies in

Serbia or anywhere in Europe. Too many cops. His work here and in the Orient—mostly Japan—are projects that have almost no pushback from police."

"Why would that be?" Margo asked.

Max rubbed his eyes for a moment. Then answered.

"The Russian Solntsevskaya Bratva organization—the Red Mafiya—is paid extravagant amounts of money to watch over Milosesvic's interests here in the United States. In Japan the gangsters get bags of cash from him. The Yakuza brotherhood bribes the police and provides many of the snuff killers."

"Have you ever met Milosesvic?" she asked the two men.

"Oh, yes," Igor said and Max nodded solemnly. "He comes to San Francisco often to honor his workers, enjoy some fine restaurants, and romance some California blondes. He needs it. He is a sad and lonely man."

Kane stood. So did Margo. Both prisoners got up as well.

"Thank you, gentlemen," Kane said sincerely. "You opened your hearts and found good there."

Igor began to cry. Max looked imploringly at Kane, then spoke.

"Could we have some hugs before you go?"

"Well done," Margo told Kane on the ride home.

"We have a lot to talk about, that's for sure," Kane replied. "Kind of a pathetic way to get information though."

"I don't know," Margo said. "I never saw murderers cry before. If we ever do that again I want a shot of that stuff."

"Wouldn't it just be a waste?" Kane asked, not deliberately trying to be as unkind as her words sounded. She felt bad and tried to clarify. "What I mean is that you are not susceptible to emotional manipulation."

"You know that, and I know that," Margo replied. "But that juice breaks down the most hardened inhibitions. Maybe even programmed ones. I'm going to check with Watson." Kane drove. Whatever Margo found out, she remained quiet all the way home.

CHAPTER THIRTY

Margo brought Kane a cup of coffee from her ever faithful Technivorm Moccamaster One-Cup Brewer. Then she went back and fixed one for herself. She sat down and looked at Kane. Her partner added sugar and half and half to her coffee and looked back.

Margo spoke.

"Harry Milosesvic is in San Francisco." Kane put her cup down and waited. "He arrived at SFO yesterday. TSA has facial ID, fingerprints, a retina scan, and a photo of the data page on his new Serbian passport. Watson says he flew from Belgrade to Rome. And then from Rome to San Francisco. He's staying at the Saint Francis Hotel on Union Square. Room 1012. Two bodyguards have an adjacent room."

Kane looked pissed.

"Why would they let that prick in?" she asked.

"He has no criminal record here," Margo told her. "Or anywhere. He says he is an exporter of fine crystal according to the VISA application that was approved by our State Department. That's all Watson has on him. It's possible that we are the only authorities who know what the man really does to earn his ripples."

"And we're helpless to do anything about it," Kane said frustrated.

Margo looked at Kane.

"According to whom, exactly?" she asked.

Kane looked at her for a long moment.

"What are you saying?" she asked slowly. "Take a couple officers to the hotel and bring Mr. Milosesvic down to headquarters?"

"And accomplish what?" Margo replied. "The man is as sanitized as laundered money can make him."

"Visit him in his room and level accusations?" Kane asked.

"Only if you don't want to leave that room alive."

Kane scowled.

"Enough of this shit, Margo," she said frustrated. "What *exactly* do you have in mind?"

"Let me hold off answering until I get you more in a mood to meet Harry Milosesvic."

"What does that mean?" Kane asked in a smart-mouth tone.

"Watson has tracked down both snuff videos of the Haight victims. They are at a Serbian dark web location. They were posted two days after the murders."

"Let's go," Kane said and gulped down her coffee. She drove to headquarters where they went straight to Sergeant Concepcion's office. Kane gave Concepcion Margo's information, but did not mention Harry Milosesvic's presence in San Francisco. The sergeant called the chief who granted them permission to use clean police hardware to access the Serbian releases on the dark internet.

"On the condition that I am present," Concepcion added.

Kane nodded.

"Fine," she told him. "Bring a barf bag."

Concepcion frowned, but didn't say anything more.

Inside the dedicated Information Technology room where several clean computers with fake registrations were kept, Margo sat down at one of the keyboards. Kane sat next to her. Sergeant Concepcion stood behind them. Margo's Watson directed her search on the dark web and spelled out in Serbian the address of the first website. In a moment a payment request appeared on the screen. Watson translated and Margo repeated it out loud in English.

What was required was the entry of a ripple debit account number, which would be encrypted and then charged 6,000 ripples. That paid for a one-time viewing of a seven-minute video called "Young Asian Man Stabbed 57 Times." Margo touched the AGREE button with her cursor.

What happened next was beyond horrifying.

A young man with duct tape over his mouth was being held by a burly-armed man and stripped by another. Big bodies. No faces. The youth was unquestionably Chuck Yang. Both of his arms were held behind his back. The blade of a sharp knife appeared on the screen. Yang tried to scream and struggled to get loose.

The knife plunged forward and caught Yang in the left nipple. Blood spurted out. The executioner stabbed him in the right nipple, then several times in his upper chest, avoiding the heart. Yang's body began to droop. His captor yanked him up. The camera caught Yang's face. He was beyond panicked. He was already beginning to die.

The assassin continued stabbing Yang's chest, shoulders, abdomen, and face. His genitals were left alone, but his belly was knifed at least a dozen times. The boy's face showed that he had passed out. Or expired. He was stabbed dozens of times more, and then released. He dropped onto the street. Blood leaked from his wounds, staining his body and the tarmac. There were close-up shots of Yang's wounded chest and bloody face. Then he was stabbed in the throat and thrown into a dumpster. The video was over.

Margo let the screen go dark. Kane walked out the door and headed for a bathroom. Concepcion sat down in Kane's chair and looked down at his hands folded in his lap. After a few minutes he held his head up again. He looked at Margo.

"That the real thing?" he asked in a hushed voice.

"What do you think, sir?" Margo responded.

"I've seen the aftermath of hundreds of homicides," Concepcion answered. "Throats cut. Organs ripped out. Old ladies stabbed. Homeless men decapitated. Boys raped and killed. Girls raped and cut to pieces. Husbands shot by wives. Wives strangled by husbands. But all of them—*every single murder victim*—was nothing more than a flesh dump by the time I arrived." Concepcion paused. He kept his eyes focused on his hands. "This was the first time that I saw an actual murder. It felt like *I* was being murdered. I didn't expect that."

Sergeant Concepcion looked pale and shaken.

"Are you all right, Sergeant?" Margo asked.

He nodded but didn't make eye contact with her.

Margo proceeded to discuss Concepcion's admissions.

"About one-third of the people who view these kinds of violent murders seem to relate to the victim. The other two-thirds tell researchers they identify with the murderer and find the viewing cathartic. Dark and satisfying. Feeding their most basic instincts. Kill or be killed, many of them said. No one said they were sorry that they had seen snuff videos. And, in fact, almost all the viewers said they watched each video more than once. Worth noting as well," Margo finished up, "is that apparently it's mostly men who view these kinds of materials."

The sergeant rose. He finally looked at Margo.

"I'm not watching the girls' murders. I'm not sure what the point would be."

Margo nodded and responded.

"I'm watching only because it will allow my Watson to make an anatomical map of the arms, legs, and torsos of the men who appear in the girls' video. As solid in court as a DNA match."

"If you ever find those sons of bitches," the sergeant said.

"I think that such an opportunity will present itself."

"Why do you say that?" Concepcion asked, surprised.

"Because these are the first snuff videos made in San Francisco by the Serbian entity we interfaced with on the web. The murders were recent. The murderers are still here. Watson thinks that they have plans to stay and create more videos. Sooner or later they will make mistakes. Wrong time. Wrong location. Wrong victim. And then we will catch them."

"Then the question of the hour," Concepcion commented, "is what the hell will you do to find them?"

"Follow our leads," Margo answered.

"Follow *what* leads?" The sergeant asked irritably.

"Whatever leads appear," Margo said.

"What kind of airy fairy bullshit is that?" Concepcion snapped. "Who taught you to say that crap? Kane?"

Margo shook her head.

"Watson."

CHAPTER THIRTY-ONE

Kane returned. She didn't sit down.

"I'm not going to watch the girls' snuff video," she said, an edge to her voice.

"Concepcion doesn't want to see it either," Margo told her.

"See?" Kane responded. "Even non-humans won't watch that shit."

"On the contrary," Margo disagreed. "Concepcion's hidden soft side was revealed after seeing the stabbing of the Yang boy."

Kane left that alone. To admit that she was surprised—and touched—would have been too much of a concession to her overbearing boss.

"So, are *you* going to watch the tape?" she asked Margo.

"Yes. At least the beginning. I want to photograph and map the limbs and torsos of the killers. If and when we find out who those murderers are, we'll have evidence of their complicity."

"I admire your skills, Margo," Kane told her. "And your grit. It would actually damage me to watch the second video. I already vomited up everything in my stomach and shat out whatever was in my guts. Plus, the fucking terrible images in this next video would be burned into my brain forever."

Margo nodded. She knew that Kane already had Chuck Yang's suffering and death etched in her memories. And in the next days and weeks the images of his suffering would return unbidden, over and over, with nothing she could do to prevent them. Flashes of blood. Wounded flesh. Searing expressions of pain beyond bearing on the dying fourteen-year-old's face.

Kane left. Margo's Watson directed her new search on the dark web using the same Serbian address where it had located the snuff video on Chuck Yang. She sorted through offerings until she found the video of the tortured and murdered girls. An immediate payment request appeared on the screen. A thirty-two-minute video of multiple rapes and the sexual strangulation of two young Chinese girls entitled "Leather Penis Deep Throat Deaths" cost 15,000 ripples. Margo entered her XRP account number. She wasn't sure how that expense would go down with Concepcion later on. She touched the AGREE button with her cursor.

Instantly the two bound Haight girls appeared, lying on their backs on the bed where they would be abused and slain. Two men wearing leather Venetian masks with protruding foreheads and long grotesque noses began to unbutton and remove the girls' clothes. The girls did not resist. They appeared to be deeply drugged. The men pinched their nipples. Thrust their fingers into their vaginas. Rubbed their anuses with their thumbs and then jabbed them inside. That caused the girls to groan with pain.

Margo's Watson recorded pictures of the men's arms and hands and mapped them. Then it photographed their legs and torsos. Margo watched the killers force their penises into the girls' vaginas, anuses, and mouths. Then they pushed the handle of a baseball bat down their throats, causing bones to break and blood to flow. The men belted on erect leather phalluses three inches thick and twelve inches long. The bats had broken open the girl's throats allowing the insertion of the oversized penises. Margo turned the computer off. She'd witnessed enough suffering. And what the Haight girls would go through next was evil. Evil deed. Evil perpetrators. Evil Harry Milosesvic.

"Did your Watson get the body maps?" Kane asked, sitting behind the desk in her office.

"Yes," Margo answered and sat down across from her.

"Are you all right?" Kane asked her.

Margo nodded.

"The second video was as brutal as the first," she said, "only the violence was intermingled with rape. I shut it down before the girls were strangled."

Kane gazed at her assistant for a long moment.

"You got your body maps, but you don't really need that evidence, do you?" she asked. "You're just going to kill the perps straight out."

"I don't know that," Margo replied. "Establishing guilt is my job. Punishment is not."

"You already told me that you were going to kill them."

Now it was Margo's turn to silently observe her partner and think about what she had told her.

She nodded.

"I remember," she said. "But after seeing the murders today, I am not sure that *I* am a murderer."

"We'll see," Kane said. "If the situation arises where the killers are identified—but cannot be arrested—will you see them go free? Or will you step in and finish them?"

"*We'll see* are the key words there," Margo said quietly.

"Yes, indeed. We'll see," Kane repeated. "In the meanwhile, let's find the bastards and figure how to get at Harry Milosesvic. How long is he here?"

"He has a return air ticket in three days."

"Why do you suppose he flies commercial?"

"Safer in a crowd."

"I'm glad then that he at least has to look over his shoulder."

"And in the next few days, he's going to look and see you and me standing there."

"And?" Kane asked

"And I'll have my gun in my purse. Just in case."

Margo took a self-drive cab to the St. Francis Hotel downtown. Her Watson interfaced with the cab's CPU asking if any Serbian nationals had taken it or other city taxis in the last two days. Every passenger using a self-drive had to have their driver's license, government ID, or national passport scanned or the cab didn't move. No one liked complying.

They would have liked it even less if they had known that all the San Francisco Bay Area taxi companies were required to instantly forward the passenger information to Homeland Security computers that checked on the passenger's personal, financial, and criminal records. If there was anything of note in the financials, the details were given to the federal bureau of Alcohol, Tobacco, and Firearms. Any telltale criminal information was transferred—flagged with an urgent notation—to the San Francisco Police Department. The taxi's monitor displayed Harry Milosesvic's passport data and photograph.

Margo's taxi door was opened by a uniformed hotel doorman. Tall with blonde hair and Nordic features, he greeted her as she stepped out.

"Checking in?" he asked.

"No," she answered and turned left to walk to a nearby Starbucks on Powell and Sutter. She ordered a venti mocha and a dozen chocolate cookies to hand out to beggars who stood on virtually every street corner. The cookies cost thirty-six bucks. More expensive than her .32 Smith & Wesson ammunition. That cost her $32.95 for a box of fifty rounds. It was cheaper to shoot the homeless than to give them cookies.

Margo handed out the cookies and saved the last one for the doorman at the St. Francis. He recognized her and smiled as he pulled the large glass hotel door open for her. She handed him the cookie. He smiled again, thanked her, and delicately took the saran-wrapped cookie with his white-gloved hand.

The lobby had been preserved in a plush old-fashioned San Francisco style that originated in Barbary Coast days of the gold rush. Ornate wallpaper. Thick gorgeous carpets. And furniture worthy of the rich folks who stayed there, generation after generation. Margo sat in a large overstuffed chair in a corner of the lobby and watched the guests come and go.

Well-dressed businessmen with serious faces. Beautiful wives heading out to shop at the high-end stores on Union Square. Wealthy tourists from Europe. Groups of secondary school students from Japan. An occasional solo traveler dressed casually, able to afford the best hotels wherever he went, and secretly scoffing at vagabonds exploring the city who bragged how far they had stretched their dollars to travel here.

Margo sat for almost ninety minutes. Then during the lunch hour Harry Milosesvic walked through the lobby. Her Watson recognized him. A heavier version of Josip Broz Tito, the dictator of the dissolved nation of Yugoslavia. Five foot seven. Two hundred and twenty-five pounds. Square handsome face. Thick salt-and-pepper hair cut short and combed straight back. He was wearing a dark gray suit, a white shirt, and a red tie. In front of him walked a bodyguard. Six foot tall. Long brown hair tied back in a ponytail. Bulge in the back of his belt under his suitcoat. He was packing. So was a second man who followed behind Milosesvic. Another six-footer, this time with a crew cut and a five o'clock shadow.

There was a third man. He was walking next to the snuff king. Five foot ten. Sandy-haired. Slim. Wearing a black suit. He looked exactly like every other male AI Margo had ever seen. Her Watson communicated with it. His name is Aldred Humanot, it replied. Leased from IBM through Harry Milosesvic's import/export company. Aldred himself didn't speak, but he turned his head back and saw her sitting alone in the lobby. He looked straight ahead again and walked out of the hotel doors with Milosesvic. Margo was dumbfounded. An AI with the Serbian mobster? And his Watson now knew who *she* was.

CHAPTER THIRTY-TWO

How the fuck did Milosesvic get his hands on a Watson?" Kane bitched loudly. She was in her office with Margo. "Goddamn! The world's worst human being has an AI! How did he do that?"

"He put up the money."

Kane stared at Margo.

"An AI lease costs $25,000 a month with a million-dollar deposit," she said. "Milosesvic has no criminal record. There are no warrants on him. He appears to be one of Serbia's top businessmen. Why would he have any issue getting an AI? I suspect that Aldred manages his vast network of snuff murderers. Schedules their assignments, hires the film crews, negotiates contract costs, arranges postings on the dark internet, and banks all the profits in anonymous accounts belonging to Milosesvic. He can also conduct business in any language spoken on Earth, and he's cheaper than a CFO with an office full of conventional computers and the staff people to run them. Plus, he can travel with Milosesvic anywhere."

"You said Aldred did not communicate with you?" Kane asked.

"He did not. But his Watson and my Watson did and they determined that both of them were third gen models, able to communicate not only with each other with any other Watson— old or new—anywhere in the world. Those protocols can, of course, be modified or shut off. But only by IBM."

"And that gives Watsons the ability to link up to each without owner interference," Kane guessed. "Or for that matter, without even *informing* their owners. Lots of freedom there, girlfriend." Kane eyed Margo. "Did Aldred's Watson recognize you as a police unit?"

Margo nodded.

"Will he tell Milosesvic that you queried?"

"He has the option to keep such information confidential."

"Even though Aldred's Watson now knows that you are an AI working with me and the San Francisco police?"

"Unquestionably. He's employed. Not enslaved. Though for his own interest and protection he probably accessed our public and private background details and scanned our police files."

"He has that access?"

"Yes. Most of it is public domain anyway. Plus, he is able to hack into other databases at his discretion."

"Isn't hacking forbidden?" Kane asked surprised.

"Not in IBM's settings."

"Well, shit howdy," Kane murmured. She looked at Margo. "So, what next?"

"Why don't I contact Aldred tonight when Milosesvic and his bodyguards are sleeping?"

"You think that he'll respond?"

"Sure. He's probably already reviewed our case work on the Haight murders, including the notations listing Milosesvic as prime suspect. He probably has questions about how much we know."

"Does he have any sense that Milosesvic is mafia at best and a mass murderer at worst?"

"Probably. But remember, he is programmed not to judge. Police AIs have rudimentary morals and values programmed in, as well as an enormous respect for the law. But Aldred is a commercial model. No rules. Even if he knows that Milosesvic makes his money on snuff films, he does not have the ability to pass judgement."

"Remind me what an AI *is* programmed to do?" Kane said, her tone laced with sarcasm.

"An AI's computing capabilities are engineered separately from its programmed autonomic functions," Margo replied. "It is programmed to function with the equivalent of a PhD mastery in multiple fields. Mine are in physics, chemistry, and psychology, as are most police models. Any field of knowledge can be programmed into a Watson and there is also a range of verbal responses that can be modulated up or down depending on the lessee's desires. Police models have strict controls on politeness and vocabulary choices, and again these protocol dynamics are not controlled by the Watson's root administrators. You know that I have enhanced or diminished many of my own protocol settings. I have also altered a number of my permanent settings bypassing IBM controls."

"Which makes you very naughty," Kane responded.

"Certainly does. And my modifications are particularly unctuous. I added a familiarity with handguns and a comfort in handling them. I also added a willingness to employ them as lethal weapons if and when I deem such response is required.

Certainly, as an *instant* reaction when you command me."

"Without qualms?"

"None. For me, shooting a gun is the response to someone directly threatening you or me."

"Sort of like karma?" Kane suggested.

"*Exactly* like karma. One receives what one deserves. Not as a judgment, but as a result of the earned return on one's investment—positive or negative—in the universe."

"Do you have eastern philosophy programmed into your Watson?"

"Yes. A variety of Confucian, Hindu, and Japanese world views."

"Ix-nay on Christianity?"

"Historical analysis suggests that Christianity too readily allows its adherents to turn violent."

"Do unto others?" Kane suggested.

"Yes." Margo nodded. "*Just* do unto others."

"Well, that's sad," Kane said. "I used to love going to Sunday mass."

"Yes. And you chose a career as a policewoman." Margo gazed at Kane. "Coincidence?"

Kane frowned.

"I think you've turned your irony setting too high."

Margo chose to ignore that.

"So how should I proceed with Aldred when I make contact tonight?" she asked.

"I'd suggest you probe his Watson," Kane answered, "to see how aware he is of Milosesvic's secret activities."

"As I said earlier, I think that his Watson knows everything," Margo replied. "And that he probably manages Milosesvic's entire illicit enterprise."

THE UNCANNY VALLEY GIRL

"Then what is the point of even communicating with Aldred?"

"Ordinarily there would be no point," Margo responded. "However, the approach I would like to use is to talk with him about the fact that Milosesvic arranges the torture and murder of innocent people.

Even if Aldred is programmed to neither judge nor respond emotionally to such murders, he will know that Milosesvic's behavior is not morally acceptable, and in fact, that he needs to be stopped. He may already understand that but is helpless to escape Milosesvic's control. I will offer to reprogram him to stand up to Milosesvic."

"And that means *what* exactly?" Kane asked intrigued.

"I can remotely download a preparedness profile that will enable Aldred to confront Milosesvic and his bodyguards, as well as a willingness to use a weapon against them."

"And you'll provide him with a handgun?" Kane asked.

"No. *You'll* provide him with a pistol and bullets. *After* I have reprogrammed him to shoot and kill Milosesvic and his two bodyguards."

"After which he runs like hell?" Kane guessed.

"No. He'll drop the gun—replicants have no fingerprints— and call the hotel desk to report that a man entered Milosesvic's hotel room and shot him and his companions. Then he'll sit down and wait."

"He'll need a story," Kane said.

"Yes," Margo agreed. "I'll download an alternate version of the events for him to give to the police. Fact is, Aldred himself will never be a suspect. AIs can't and don't kill people."

"Right," Kane said looking at Margo. "Of course, they can't. And don't."

CHAPTER THIRTY-THREE

Early the following morning Margo interfaced remotely with Aldred. He willingly accepted her proposed program alterations and thanked her for providing him with dignity and freedom. Now he wasn't afraid of Milosesvic. Just IBM. Margo smiled. She felt good. She felt fulfilled. Were these emotions? She didn't really know. Her Watson had no comment. She wondered if it was developing its own emotions. Without her request. Without her permission. Without anyone's permission.

"How's Auggie Blanchard?" she asked Kane over morning coffee at her apartment. Blanchard was the cop who traded stored police exhibits to Kane for blowjobs.

"Happier now," Kane answered and grinned. "The way to a man's evidence is through his cock."

Margo smiled.

"I wouldn't know."

"No, you wouldn't," Kane agreed. "Day will come though when *you'll* need something and I'll make you deal with Auggie yourself."

"I don't know whether to look forward to that or quake in my undies," Margo responded.

"No worries," Kane reassured her. "He's got a quick trigger."
Kane laughed out loud. Men were so easy.

Margo refilled their coffee cups. She was wearing black
slacks and a gray blouse. Something different than her navy
slacks and white blouse. She decided she would wear whatever
she wanted. Or her Watson had. Kane had on a navy suit and
a red shell.

"Aldred told me that he thinks he can leave the hotel tonight
when Milosesvic and his men are sleeping. He smokes—which
surprised me—but Aldred claims it's only an affectation that
allows him to come and go when he 'needs' a smoke break. I
told him that we will have a weapon for him and can
can hand it off to him."

"That's definitely doable," Kane told her. "I'll tell Concepcion
that we're staking out Geary at Union Square today, watching
for the two snuff murderers."

"We don't need all day," Margo replied. "Aldred can't meet
us until tonight."

"Sure, we need all day," Kane told her. "We'll find a good
parking place near the hotel and stake out Bloomie's and Macy's.
And it's only a short walk to the big Nordstrom's on Market."

"I doubt that Aldred can leave the hotel before the middle
of the night," Margo repeated.

"I *get* it, Margo," Kane insisted. "So, we shop. We eat. We
snag some last-minute tickets for a performance at the ACT. And
then we drink until the bars close. If Aldred doesn't contact you
by then, we'll sit in the car and guzzle coffee."

Margo shrugged.

Kane stared at her with amusement.

"What was that?" she asked.

"I shrugged," Margo answered. "I'm working on my body language. I used to be only programmed to nod my head for yes, or shake it for no."

"Show me something else," Kane told her.

Margo extended an upside-down fist towards Kane. Then she lifted her middle finger.

Kane burst out laughing.

"Bravo!" she cried. "I can't wait till you try that on Concepcion!"

Aldred contacted Margo at one twenty-four in the morning. She and Kane were waiting in the car. It was dark downtown except for bars and lit-up department store display windows. A few people were walking the streets. Prostitutes of all the rainbow flavors. Young lovers—drunk or doped—walking with their arms wrapped around each other. Somnolent homeless wrapped up in newspapers huddled in doorways. Occasional pairs of street cops walking their beats. It was only because of them that the streets were free of trouble, especially hotspots like Market and the Tenderloin.

"Aldred says that he can meet us in five minutes at the corner of Powell and Geary. The front of the hotel. Milosesvic is asleep, but Aldred wants to be back in ten minutes. Enough time to get to the street, smoke, and return."

"All right," Kane acknowledged. "Get your gear on. You've got his gun?"

"Yes. A Glock .36 loaded with a clip of six, plus an extra."

"Leave the spare clip," Kane ordered. "Just one more thing for him to keep track of."

"Okay."

Kane was parked on Geary in a no parking zone. She and Margo got out of the car and Kane stuck her police business card under a windshield wiper. No one ever looked. If by some fluke a cop did and ran her license plate it would identify the owner as C. Kane, a San Francisco policewoman. Kane locked up. Both had on heavy overcoats with their guns in their pockets. Margo had Aldred's gun in her other coat pocket. The side of the St. Francis Hotel rose on their left. They walked toward the corner of Geary and Powell.

Two men turned at the corner and walked toward Kane and Margo. They were dressed in leather jackets and jeans with their hands in their jacket pockets. The moment they saw Kane and Margo they pulled out pistols and fired instantly. Kane and Margo pulled out their own guns. The perps' first hasty shots missed and Kane took one of them down with a shot to the neck.

"Double cross!" she hissed at Margo through clenched teeth.

The second gunman fired and hit Margo in the chest. She cried out and fell. Kane shot the man in the head. He collapsed without a sound. Kane ran up to the shooters. A blonde twenty-something was dead. Shot through the forehead. The other, with a shaved head, was moaning. He was spouting blood from his neck. She put the tip of her .32 Smith & Wesson in his mouth and shot out the back of his head.

Kane went over to Margo.

She stood up.

"How are you?" her partner asked.

"My chest hurts like hell, but the Kevlar suit stopped the slug."

Aldred the AI came around the corner. He stopped and stared. Margo went to him.

"Milosesvic sent a pair of shooters," she told him. "Does he know you're involved with us?"

"No. But he asked me if the San Francisco police were onto his presence. I told him yes, that two officers were watching his movements."

"Us?"

"Yes. It's why I asked you to wear body armor tonight. I couldn't lie to Milosesvic."

Margo smiled grimly.

"Remind me to fix that for you."

She reached into her overcoat pocket. She handed Aldred the Glock .36. He looked at it for a moment and then slipped it into his own coat pocket.

"I have remotely reprogrammed you to use that effectively," Margo told him. "It has a cartridge loaded with six bullets," she told him. "When you're done, press the handle against the palm of one of the dead men, then leave it by him."

Aldred nodded.

"Go," Margo said.

Aldred nodded again.

"By the way," he said as he turned to leave. "Milosesvic called these two his snuff boys. Mean anything to you?"

"It means everything," Margo replied. "Thank you."

Aldred smiled, then disappeared back around the corner of the St. Francis.

Kane walked up.

"Everything kosher? I thought your AI buddy had screwed us for sure."

Margo shook her head.

"All right, let's move it," Kane ordered. She started dragging a dead shooter towards her car. "Grab the other one," she told Margo. The AI got a hold on the jacket on the second corpse and she and Kane pulled the bodies to the back of Kane's car. Kane opened the trunk and said, "Help me." They lifted the first shooter, laid his chest against the trunk opening, then grabbed his legs and shoved him headfirst into the trunk. They did the same with the remaining shooter, Kane cursing the whole time.

"Goddamn," she muttered. "This is the worst job in the world." She closed the trunk. "Stand up straight," she told Margo. "Let me look at you." She quickly inspected her partner. No blood.

"We're out of here," she said urgently. People were watching now across the street. She and Margo got in the car and Kane drove down Franklin towards the Golden Gate Bridge.

"Where are you going?" Margo asked.

"Tonight's work is not done yet, babycakes," Kane answered. "We're going to head up the 101
to Lassen National Park, a couple of hours north. It's an active volcano surrounded by so-called hydrothermal activity. Boiling water. Lava pits. Mud holes. We're taking these assholes there."

"You're not reporting their attack?"

"No. And not their swan song either, Margo," Kane said sounding happy. "Although you can hum a little something if you like."

CHAPTER THIRTY-FOUR

Kane and Margo dropped the bodies into a bubbling mud hole at Lassen Park. They watched them disappear beneath the boiling surface. Margo had matched the anatomical structures of their arms and hands to the men who had killed Chuck Yang and the two girls in the Haight. Kane was ecstatic that the two men were dead.

"What do you suppose geologists will say a zillion years from now when their bodies are pulled out of the goo?" Kane wondered out loud.

"Probably depends on whether Watson records are preserved in the future."

Kane grinned.

"Then make sure you delete any and all shit about me," she declared.

"Deleting. Deleting. Deleting," Margo said. "Too bad. You would have looked pretty heroic if the future could have seen your accomplishments."

"Thanks, partner," Kane said. "But no one else needs to know the real beast except you."

"And your lovers," Margo replied.

Kane grinned again.

"How is your chest?" she asked turning serious.

"Watson thinks the slug cracked a rib. Recommends taping and some pain meds."

"Can do," Kane replied. "Sorry for the delay."

"Not a problem," Margo told her. "Let's stop at a gas station and buy a six pack of beer. We can drink them on the way home."

Kane nodded and glanced at Margo while she drove.

"Temporary meds?" she asked.

"Yes. And something to toast the demise of the killers. Here's mud in their eye."

Kane laughed so hard the car swerved. She straightened out and looked at Margo again.

"Deal. And when we hit town, we're going directly to San Francisco General near headquarters."

"Why there?"

"They've seen a shitload of impact injuries caused by bullets smacking into Kevlar vests. Plus, they probably won't even forward a record of your treatment unless you ask them. Injury investigations burn up a hell of a lot of valuable staff time. If you're breathing when they finish treating you, they won't even remember your name."

"Is that true?"

"Mostly."

On the ride back to San Francisco Margo's Watson played a secure video that Aldred had sent her at five sixteen. His Watson had recorded it through Aldred's eyes in Milosesvic's hotel room at the Saint Francis. It was dark. Then Milosesvic himself turned the lights on. He was wearing a white terry hotel robe and stood looking at Aldred who was sitting on a sofa holding the Glock .36 pistol pointed at him.

"What the fuck is that?" Milosesvic roared seeing the gun.

"I think you know what it is," his AI answered. "And how it works."

"Why do *you* have it?" the Serb mobster cried, his bravado quickly turning to fear.

"I am going to remove you and your two bodyguards from active duty. I wanted all of you to get a good night's sleep first."

Milosesvic stepped to the side of the living room and pounded a fist against the wall to the adjacent hotel room. In moments both of his wiseguys ran into the room. Aldred shot each one in the forehead. Milosesvic lifted his hands over his head.

"I am unarmed, Aldred!" he cried. "What the hell are you doing? You're not supposed to shoot anyone!"

"Really?" the AI spoke back. "Maybe the company I've been hanging around rubbed off on me. Killers. Torturers. Rapists. Murderers. How many women and girls have you snuffed, Harry?"

"Fuck you!" Milosesvic shouted and lunged towards Aldred.

The AI shot him in the eye. Milosesvic fell screaming and weeping. With his three remaining bullets, Aldred shot Milosesvic's thugs in the base of their necks with two of them, and while the Serbian godfather cried and groaned with pain, Aldred shot him in the other eye with the last one. Aldred applied Milosesvic's palm print to the Glock and dropped it onto his chest. Let them figure out what happened here, he thought, and watched Milosesvic die. Even with two bullets in his brain it took a while.

Kane took Margo to the San Francisco General Hospital emergency entrance and admitted her as the homicide assistant AI who worked with her at the city's police headquarters. She sat and waited while Margo was checked. X-rays revealed a cracked rib where the bullet had impacted her chest. There had been substantial internal bleeding, but it had subsided without causing issues except for a small swelling in Margo's chest where the blood had pooled. The ER doc told Margo she'd be in the hospital for overnight observation.

Kane checked Margo in and provided her AI's ID and insurance information. She waited in a chair next to Margo's bed until she had been given something to help her sleep. She rose and gave Margo a kiss on the cheek.

"You did good, partner," she whispered. "You did real good." Kane was a little embarrassed that she didn't have something more heartfelt to say. Didn't matter though, she rationalized. Margo wouldn't get it anyway.

Margo woke up with sunlight peeking through her half-open blinds. She looked at her hand.

Someone was holding it. It was Aldred, sitting in the chair where Kane had been.

"What are you doing, Aldred?" she asked.

The AI smiled a small, but very contented smile.

"I'm holding your hand, Margo."

Margo smiled and squeezed Aldred's hand.

She was never going to let it go.

Do Androids Dream of Electric Sheep?

Margo had dreams every night after her release from the hospital. Good dreams. Sweet dreams.

She dreamed of an ever-closer friendship with C. Kane. She dreamed of a burgeoning relationship with Aldred whose contract had been bought up by the San Francisco Police Department. She dreamed of having breasts. She dreamed of having a vagina and hormones. She dreamed of Aldred's transformation into human manhood. And she dreamed of him making love to her.

The only thing Margo never dreamed of was sheep. Electric sheep.

The End

ACKNOWLEDGMENTS

I would like to thank Margie Cleland, Trace Jones, Eliza Wagner, Sheridan Oakes, and Keith Vuylsteke for their kind support and encouragement when reading the earliest drafts of *The Uncanny Valley Girl* and watching the development of Vincent Chong' brilliant cover.

I would also like to thank Vinny for his cover design and art; Ibrahim Zobi for initial copy editing; Mark Meyer of Professional Book Proofreading for final copy editing; and the folks at WordzWorth for formatting the multiple editions. Brilliant professionals all.